San Juan Classics II
COOKBOOK

Dawn Ashbach
Janice Veal

Northwest Island Associates
Anacortes Washington

Printed in the United States of America
Second printing

Cover photograph of Cattle Point, San Juan Island by Eric A. Kessler
Title lettering by Nancy Jang

By the authors: *San Juan Classics Cookbook*, *San Juan Classics II Cookbook*, and *Adventures in Greater Puget Sound*—an educational guide and activity book exploring the marine environment of Greater Puget Sound. All are available from Northwest Island Associates at the address above.

Library of Congress Cataloging-In-Publication Data
Library of Congress Catalog Card Number 97-95080
Ashbach, Dawn, 1948-
    San Juan Classics II
    Includes index.
    1. Cookery–Washington (State)–San Juans
I. Janice Veal, 1947   .II Title.
641.5
ISBN 0-9629778-1-0

Table of Contents

Dedication

We dedicate this cookbook to our extraordinary families who have provided us with their support, patience and healthy appetites. Thank you for your genuine kindness and love: Bud, Matt and Brian Ashbach and Glen, Adam and Eric Veal.

Preface

Nestled in the cold waters of the Pacific Northwest lie the San Juan Islands. The bounty of the land and surrounding sea provide the natural ingredients to create fresh, mouthwatering flavors. San Juan Classics II offers a unique blend of cuisines reflecting the rich abundance of the region and the creative talents of people who love good food.

After 10 years of success with our first cookbook, we have created this book to reflect new cooking styles and feature new restaurants and chefs of the region. It is an eclectic collection of over 250 recipes that range from quick and healthy to complex and decadent. It retains the spirit of our first edition, melding Northwest fare with classic ethnic dishes including recipes from Dungeness Crab with Lemon Risotto to Grilled Steak with Peppercorn Sauce, we have combined the best of the old and new.

Before you turn to the recipes, we urge you to read the following introduction by Peter Capen. From his experience in the islands and his particular interest as a naturalist, he has put together a word picture of the San Juan Islands that beautifully captures the essence of the islands. In such a setting, it seems only natural that cooks would be inspired by the bounty that surrounds them.

Restaurants

Our thanks to the chefs and proprietors of these outstanding restaurants for generously sharing their talents and expertise with us in the production of San Juan Classics Cookbook II.

SAN JUAN ISLAND
Downriggers on the Waterfront
Duck Soup Inn
Friday Harbor House
Front Street Cafe
Katrina's
Maloula Restaurant
Mariella Inn
Roberto's
Roche Harbor Restaurant
The Place Next to the San Juan Ferry Cafe

ORCAS ISLAND
Cafe Olga
Chimayo
Christina's
Garden Cafe
La Famiglia Ristorante
Orcas Hotel
Rosario Resort
Ships Bay Oyster House
Turtleback Farm Inn

LOPEZ ISLAND
Holly B's Bakery
The Bay Cafe

FIDALGO ISLAND
Anacortes Brewhouse
Bella Isola
Calico Cupboard Old Town Cafe
    and Bakery
Geppetto's
Gere-a-Deli
La Petite Restaurant
La Vie en Rose
Star Bar
The Salmon Run Bistro

SKAGIT VALLEY
Calico Cupboard Cafe and Bakery
Courtyard Cafe
Deli Next Door
LaConner Brewing Company
Rhododendron Cafe

Acknowledgements

We would like to express our heartfelt gratitude to our generous families and friends who have encouraged and supported us in the development of this, our second cookbook. In the years it has taken us to produce this book we have had the good fortune to meet many gifted chefs, bakers and cooks. Their generous contributions have helped create this special collection. We feel fortunate to include the introduction by naturalist Peter Capen. We are indebted to our friend and computer guru Joseph Miller whose expertise guided us in production. Thanks to Nora Kembar, whose editing insured clarity and consistency. Our profound gratitude to our photographers for sharing their exquisite pictures of the San Juan Islands: Kathleen Brown, Matt Brown, Peter D. Capen, Eric Kessler, Joella Solus, Claude Steeleman and Vince Streano.

Our sincere thanks to the following chefs and bakers who generously shared recipes: Mark Abrahamson, Rich Aguilar, Steve Anderson, Gretchen Allison, Greg Atkinson, Tim Barrette, Derek Beck, Holly Bower, Raymond and Patty Brogi, Yuriko Bullock, Jodi Calhoun, Roberto Carrieri, Andrew Ferguson, Susan Fletcher, Linda Freed, Laurie Gere, James Harper, Christian Hogle, Mark Iverson, Georgia Johnson, Kathy Longstreet, Marcy Lund, Michael Magerkurth, Kathy Mohrweiss, Nassarallah Family, Christina Orchid, Laurie Paul, Bill Ray, Craig Sanders, David Schultze, Don and Carol Shank, Bill Shaw, Chuck Silva and Karen Campbell Silva, Mike Stark, Kate Stone, Kevin Sykes, Laura and Bill Thomas, Carol Tilghman, Robert Wood, Todd Wood and Libi Zderic.

We thank our friends and cooks extrordinaire for sharing their favorite recipes: Zobra Anasazi, Bud Ashbach, Claudia Ashbach, Lee Ashbach, Pete Augusztiny, Dorothy Bird, June Bisordi, Cleo Bratt, Al Bush, Paula Clancey, Pat DeStaffany, Dixon Elder, Sue Fellner, Carol Foster, Olga Gorman, Sam and Kim Haines, Dianne Hanlon, Mike Hardy, Sandy Harper, Art Hyatt, Patty Johnson, Ingrid Stahlbrand Kassler, Marianne Mach, Anne McCracken, Mary O'Hern, Linda Porter, Sharron Prosser, Dick and Kathy Robinson, Jan and Mike Russillo, Mike Smith, Linda Spicher, Dean Thompson, Connie Walser, Sandy Warmouth and Doreen Wickline. Not only does it take a village to raise a child, but it takes a host of talented individuals to create a book, thank you all.

The San Juan Islands

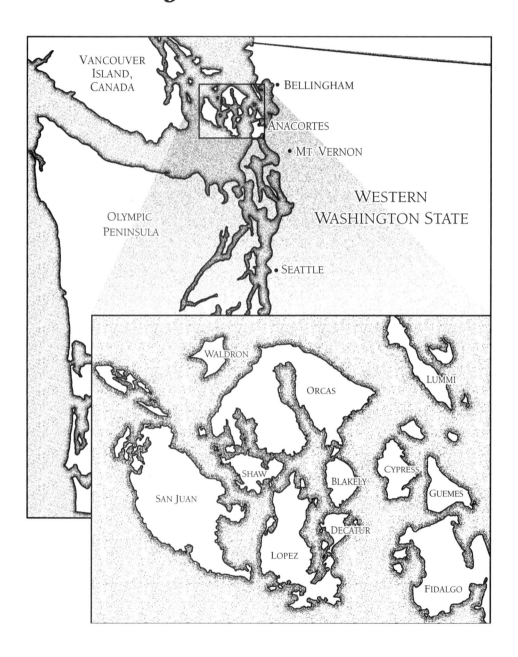

Introduction

by Peter D. Capen

A decade has passed since I left the San Juans. Yet my memories are as fresh today, as if I had never left. I am not sure that anyone who has experienced intimately the beauty and magic of the islands can ever truly leave them. The place becomes woven into the warp and weave of your soul. Despite the passage of time, every year I find the islands beckoning me back. Mostly now I return in summer to lead natural history seminars, to talk about the extraordinary marine life that dwells in the surrounding waters, or about the pods of sleek and powerful orcas, old friends that cruise Haro Strait in search of the returning runs of salmon heading home to spawn in their natal streams in the Fraser, Skagit, and other rivers that drain into the Strait of Georgia and Greater Puget Sound. Seeing these rocky, forested islands, sometimes glistening in a sparkling sunlit sea, sometimes shrouded in a misty rain, I know I am home again.

The ferry chugs smoothly through the glassy, emerald green water. Here and there a salmon leaps free of the surface, only to drop back with an ungainly splash and disappear without a trace. A jellyfish pulsates near the surface, carried along by the strong flow of the current. Startled, a small group of dark brown Rhinoceros Auklets bobbing up and down on the water scramble to get their plump, bullet-shaped bodies airborne. Eventually succeeding, they wing off low over the surface, angling away from the boat. Strolling the jagged rocks along the water's edge, a Black Oystercatcher pauses among the brown, red, and green seaweeds, bends down, and slips its bright orange, knife-like bill under a limpet, deftly popping the small, single-shelled mollusk lose from its tenacious grip. Just beyond in the water, a family of river otters frolics in the kelp, searching for a tasty crab or sea cucumber. Although normally found on near streams, the San Juans' abundant river otters are often seen foraging along the shoreline and in the quiet, sheltered bays.

Further on, a bald eagle perched on a twisted snag along the shoreline watches unconcerned as the ferry drones rhythmically past. On a tree nearby, another eagle suddenly takes flight, skims low over the surface of the water, dips its razor sharp talons into the current, and with an elegant gracefulness that can only leave a fisherman in awe, effortlessly plucks out a salmon. Scarcely missing a beat of its powerful, eight-foot wingspan, the eagle flies heavily back to its tree limb to leisurely dine on its meal. It is this sheer exuberance of Nature primeval that makes the San Juans so special. The rhythms of Nature have repeated themselves in the islands all but undisturbed over the millennia, ever since the Vashon Stade, the last surge of the Fraser Glaciation, put its finishing touches on the land it had sculpted and then retreated north of the Canadian border some 10,000 years ago, leaving the sea to flow back in, swirling in powerful flooding and ebbing tides and currents that lick the shores of the rocky archipelago.

The San Juan Islands lie nestled in the "rain shadow" of the Olympic Mountains and the Strait of Juan de Fuca. Haro Strait lies to the west, the Strait of Georgia to the north, Rosario Strait and the Washington mainland to the east, and Puget Sound to the south. It is said that there are some 473 islands that make up the San Juans. This figure, however, includes not only what might be called "proper islands," but also the numerous rocks and reefs that are visible throughout the archipelago at high tide. At low tide, the number jumps even higher, to 768. If you count just the islands that are important enough to have names, the figure usually given is 172, but only 25 of these are considered "major" islands.

The four largest "rocks," as islanders affectionately call the San Juans, are Lopez, Shaw, Orcas, and San Juan. They are the only islands in the San Juans that are served by ferry. The rest you need a boat or plane to reach. At 57 square miles, horseshoe-shaped Orcas is the largest of the four. It also boasts the highest point in the San Juans, Mt. Constitution, which rises 2,409 feet. From the top of the stone look-out tower on the summit of Mt. Constitution, where winds gust up the sheer back face of the peak, there is a breathtaking 360-degree vista of the surrounding islands, and the mainland and rugged, snow-capped Cascades and towering Mount Baker across Rosario Strait. It is from this point that I once watched a merlin, that small, swift, and purposeful falcon, make a headlong diving "stoop" on some unseen and unsuspecting prey far below. While such scenes are rare elsewhere, in the San Juans they are common.

12

Hilly San Juan is the second largest island in the archipelago—at 55 square miles. The town of Friday Harbor is the county seat. This bustling village, with its busy marina and many small shops and restaurants, is also home to the marvelous Whale Museum. Visitors can spend hours at this wonderful museum, learning more about the orcas, minke whales, porpoises, and seals that feed and grow fat in the rich waters surrounding the islands. For those who want to see orcas and other marine mammals in the wild, there are regularly scheduled whale-watching boat tours out of Friday Harbor throughout summer. The whale-watching park at Lime Kiln Lighthouse on the west side of the island is a good place to observe marine mammals from land. Pods of orcas regularly pass by the park, often just off the rocky shoreline. For the more adventuresome, kayaking excursions are also available along the west side. However you see them, few experiences are more thrilling than to hear the blows of the whales and see the erect, six-foot tall dorsal fin of a large male orca slice the water as it rises majestically to the surface, or to have an orca suddenly burst from the water in a towering breach of cascading spray. No matter how many times you have seen these magnificent animals, each time is a thrill anew. Seeing orcas in the wild touches some latent, nearly forgotten part of our souls, a part that has been all but lost as the hectic pace of modern life has increasingly disconnected us from pulse of the natural world.

Lopez Island is 29 square miles, while Shaw, the smallest of the four ferry served islands, is only 4,937 acres. Lopez is characterized by gently rolling farmlands and orchards, interspersed with stands of conifer forest. The island resonates with a relaxed, laid back lifestyle from another era, a time when the islands were the home of hardy homesteaders who worked hard and thrived from the abundance that Nature offered. The soils were tillable, the shorelines and bays rich in oyster and clam beds, the water teeming with fish. Times have changed on Lopez, but much remains the same.

For Shaw, the changes have been even fewer. With limited development, no business center, save the store run by the Franciscan nuns at the ferry landing, and only a small public campground, Shaw has remained quiet, rural, and largely undisturbed. It is not surprising that the island boasts a small Great Blue Heron rookery, where these tall, almost ungainly looking birds, with their long, stilt-like legs, powerful, sharply pointed bills, and

seven-foot wingspread, can find trees that are protected from human distur-
bance and large enough in which to build their communal nests of large
stick platforms. While not a finicky eater, the heron is often found slowly
walking along the shoreline throughout the San Juans, or standing silently
on a mat of floating bull kelp offshore, poised to spear the unwary fish, crab,
or other unsuspecting small prey that ventures too close to its steady gaze
and formidable beak. When startled, the heron unceremoniously flies off
with a loud, croaking call of complaint.

Most of the San Juan Islands are uninhabited, but privately owned.
However, 84 of the rocks, reefs, grassy islets, and smaller forested islands
scattered throughout the archipelago make up the San Juan Islands National
Wildlife Refuge, home to nesting colonies of alcids, cormorants, and thousands
of pairs of Glaucous-winged Gulls, one of the largest breeding colonies of
this species on the West Coast. Here, too, are sheltered haulouts for harbor
seals and their new pups in early summer, or undisturbed nesting sites for
bald eagles in towering, old-growth Douglas firs. In the currents offshore of
these isolated islands, small groups of the little, shy and reclusive harbor
porpoise surface and dive, as they feed on the rich schools of herring and
sand lance. Although once common throughout Puget Sound, harbor
porpoise are usually only now seen in the San Juans and nearby Strait of
Juan de Fuca. Nearly everywhere throughout the islands the bottom and
rocky submarine walls teem with a myriad assortment of invertebrates,
colorful sea anemones and sponges, sea stars, some as large as three feet
across, crabs, shrimps, sea cucumbers, urchins, and gaudy-colored sea
slugs, whose brilliant hues belie their delicate vulnerability.

In addition to the islands that are part of the National Wildlife Refuge,
there are several Nature Conservancy preserves in the San Juans, as well as
various small islands that are part of the State Park system. Of the Nature
Conservancy preserves, none can compare with Yellow Island in the spring,
when the wildflowers are in full bloom. Purchased by the Conservancy in
1980, Yellow Island boasts one of the most spectacular wildflower displays
to be found in the San Juans. There are more than eighty-five species of
flowering plants on the island, including white fawn lilies, shooting stars,
Indian paintbrush, blue camas, and chocolate lilies. The bloom reaches its
peak between April and May and permission is required to visit the island.

14

Humans have long been attracted to the beauty and the abundance of nature that have blessed the San Juans for thousands of years. Long before the Spanish explorers first sighted the islands in the late 1700s, or British and American settlers landed and started building their homesteads there in the mid-1800s, the Lummi Indians considered the San Juans their ancestral home. To the Lummi, who today live on a reservation on the mainland near the city of Bellingham, the northeast shore of San Juan Island is where "First Man" dropped from the sky and founded their race in this "Garden of Eden." It is easy to understand why the Lummi saw their beginnings in the San Juans. Rich in nature and beauty, the islands are a magical place that, once experienced, inevitably draw you back again.

Peter Capen is a natural history author, lecturer and photographer. He lived in the San Juan Islands for a number of years, during which time he was Executive Director of The Whale Museum in Friday Harbor. He currently lives in Tacoma, WA, where he teaches at a community college.

Appetizers

MATT BROWN

Mosquito Pass

Bruschetta con Pomodori

This garlic bread with tomato topping has a flavor that immediately says "Italian." No wonder it has become such a popular appetizer.

    1 (8-ounce) Italian or French bread, cut into ½-inch slices
    3 cloves garlic, peeled
    Extra-virgin olive oil
    Salt and freshly ground pepper
    TOMATO TOPPING (recipe follows)

1. Preheat broiler. On a large cookie sheet, broil bread to a golden brown on one side only.

2. While bread is still hot, rub toasted side with garlic clove. Pour a thin stream of olive oil over each slice, enough to soak lightly. Season with salt and pepper.

3. Prepare Tomato Topping, according to directions below. Top each slice with 2 tablespoons Tomato Topping.

4. Arrange on a serving platter, serve while warm.   4-6 servings

TOMATO TOPPING

    1 tablespoon olive oil
    8 ripe plum tomatoes, peeled, seeded and diced
    ¼ cup minced fresh basil leaves
        or 2 teaspoons dried basil
    1 tablespoon balsamic vinegar
    Salt and freshly ground pepper, to taste

In a small saucepan, heat olive oil over medium. Add tomatoes and cook for 1-2 minutes, until heated through. Remove from heat and add remaining ingredients.   2 cups

Bruschetta with Olive Tapenade

This robust variation on our recipe for Bruschetta Con Pomodori provides an aromatic and flavorful change. The tapenade is delicious on its own as a topping for bread, pizza or pasta. It is a favorite with our family and friends during the holidays.

Olive Tapenade
  1 cup pitted calamata olives
  ¼ cup sliced black olives
  2 teaspoons balsamic vinegar
  1 tablespoon capers, drained
  1 tablespoon extra-virgin olive oil
  2 cloves garlic
TOMATO TOPPING (see page 19)
1 loaf Italian bread, cut into ½-inch slices
Parmesan Cheese

1. Prepare Olive Tapenade: In a blender or food processor, combine olives, vinegar, capers, olive oil and garlic. Blend until smooth or the texture you desire. (If made ahead, mixture can be covered and refrigerated for a week.)

2. Preheat broiler. On a large baking sheet, broil bread to a golden brown on one side only. Pour a thin stream of olive oil over each slice.

3. Prepare Tomato Topping according to directions on page 19.

4. Preheat oven to 425°. Spread each slice with tapendade; top with Tomato Topping and sprinkle with Parmesan.

5. Bake Bruschetta for 2 to 3 minutes until Parmesan is melted. Arrange on a serving platter, serve while warm.   4-6 servings

Roasted Peppers

Peppers develop a unique smoky flavor when roasted. Serve them on Bruschetta or Polenta as an appetizer. Roasted peppers also add appealing flavor and color to salads, vegetables and as an accompaniment to a meat entree.

> **6 red and yellow bell peppers**
> **2 tablespoons minced garlic**
> **3 tablespoons red wine or balsamic vinegar**
> **⅓ cup extra-virgin olive oil**
> **Salt and pepper, to taste**

1. Preheat broiler to 400°. Place the peppers on a lightly greased broiler pan. Broil peppers 5 inches from heat source, until the skin is blackened on one side. Turn to blacken all over, about 15 minutes total.

2. In a medium bowl, combine garlic, vinegar and olive oil; set aside.

3. When peppers are done, place them in a paper bag and close tightly. Let cool for 20 minutes.

4. Remove peppers from bag. Using your fingers, peel the skin from the peppers and remove stems, cores and seeds. Rinse peppers and pat dry; cut into thin strips.

5. Add peppers to olive oil mixture; toss to coat. Cover and let marinate at room temperature for 1 hour before serving. Peppers can be refrigerated for up to 1 week. Serve at room temperature.   6-8 servings

Caponata

Caponata is a traditional Italian ratatouille from Sicily. It can be served as an appetizer as part of an anitpasto plate, over bruschetta, as a salad or side dish. We fell in love with it when we first tasted it at DeLaurentis at the Pike Place Market.

1 large eggplant, unpeeled and diced
1 teaspoon salt
¼ cup extra-virgin olive oil
2 cloves garlic, minced
1 small red onion, minced
1 cup diced celery
1 red pepper, diced
2 tablespoons tomato paste
4 large plum tomatoes, peeled, seeded and chopped
2 tablespoons capers
3 tablespoons red wine vinegar
1 tablespoon sugar
½ cup calamata or green olives, chopped
¼ cup minced fresh Italian parsley
3 tablespoons minced fresh basil or 1 teaspoon dried basil

1. In a large colander, sprinkle eggplant with salt and toss. Let drain for 30 minutes. Rinse with water, drain and pat dry.

2. In a large frying pan, over medium, heat olive oil and sauté eggplant until softened. Add garlic, onion, celery, and red pepper. Cover and steam until vegetables are tender-crisp, about 10 minutes.

3. Gently combine remaining ingredients. Cover with lid ajar and simmer for 15 minutes.

4. Remove from heat, cover and refrigerate at least 8 hours. Serve at room temperature.   5 cups

Eggplant and Red Pepper Spread

Serve this exquisite, mouth watering appetizer on our Bruschetta. It will be a sure crowd pleaser.

   1 tablespoon extra-virgin olive oil
   1 clove garlic, minced
   1 eggplant, peeled and cut into ½-inch slices
   1 cup roasted red peppers*
   ½ teaspoon capers
   Salt and freshly ground pepper, to taste
   12 slices garlic toast (see Bruschetta page 19)

1. Preheat oven to 425°. In a small bowl, combine olive oil and garlic. Lightly brush each side of eggplant with oil mixture and arrange on oiled baking sheet. Bake eggplant about 10 minutes or until light brown and tender, turn and bake for 5 minutes more.

2. Coarsely chop eggplant and red peppers, and place in medium bowl. Stir in capers, salt and pepper. Cover and refrigerate if made ahead. Spread can be served warm or cold.

3. Prepare Bruschetta following recipe directions.

4. Arrange Bruschetta on platter and top with spread.

                                                        2-3 cups

Available in jars at grocery stores or see recipe for fresh Roasted Peppers on page 21.

Margarita Prawns

The building that now houses the Majestic Hotel was built in 1890, when speculators believed that Anacortes would be the "New York of the West." When visiting this beautifully restored hotel, ask for a brochure on the history of the building. Proprietor and Chef Bill Ray of the popular Salmon Run Bistro, serves these attractively presented prawns. They are enhanced by the piquant combination of peppers and citrus which highlight the sweet meat of the prawns.

ꞏ¼ cup butter
16 large fresh prawns, peeled and deveined
1 teaspoon chopped fresh garlic
2 green onions, sliced
⅛ cup chopped green bell peppers
⅛ cup chopped red bell peppers
2 fresh jalapeno chili peppers, seeded and minced
⅛ cup fresh lemon juice
⅛ cup fresh lime juice
2 tablespoons chopped fresh cilantro
¼ cup Triple Sec
¼ cup tequila
Coarse salt, garnish
Lime wedges, garnish

1. In a frying pan, over medium heat, melt butter and sauté prawns until they begin to turn pink. Add the garlic, onion and peppers and sauté until vegetables are tender. Stir in lemon and lime juice and cilantro.

2. Add Triple Sec and tequila to frying pan. Proceeding with caution, ignite alcohol. (It will flame up in a flash.)

3. To serve, use 4 margarita glasses or other long-stemmed glasses. Dip each glass rim into water, then dip rim into coarse salt. Place 4 prawns into each glass and divide sauce evenly over prawns. Garnish each glass rim with a lime wedge.   4 servings

Applewood Smoked Oysters
With Cucumber Salsa

Chef Gretchen Allison emphasizes fresh local products at her famous Duck Soup Inn on San Juan Island. Gretchen's menu changes with the coming of each season. Oysters from Westcott Bay, located down the road from the restaurant, were used to develop this recipe. If you visit San Juan Island, a visit to her fine restaurant is a definite necessity.

> **30 fresh small or medium oysters, in shell**
> **Rock salt**
> **CUCUMBER SALSA (recipe follows)**
> **⅓ cup butter**
> **½ cup freshly grated Parmesan**

1. Prepare oysters: With an oyster knife, remove and discard the top half of the shell. Rinse oysters in bottom shell in salted water (1 teaspoon kosher salt to 2 quarts water) to remove bits of shell and grit. With sharp knife, cut muscle under oyster, and flip oyster over (the underside is more attractive).

2. Using applewood chips, prepare smoker. Place oysters on rack and smoke for one hour.

3. While oysters are smoking, prepare Cucumber Salsa. Cover and set aside.

4. Preheat oven to 500°. Fill a large baking pan with 1-inch of rock salt and place oysters in the shell onto rock salt. Top each oyster with a 1/4 teaspoon of butter and sprinkle with Parmesan.

5. Bake for 4-5 minutes, or until edges of oyster begin to curl. Remove from oven and top each oyster with 2 teaspoons of Cucumber Salsa. Arrange on serving platter and enjoy!
                                                                30 oysters

CUCUMBER SALSA

1 medium cucumber, peeled, seeded and diced
¼ cup finely chopped red onion
2 tablespoons finely chopped red pepper
2 jalapeno peppers, finely chopped
2 teaspoons chopped garlic
½ teaspoon kosher salt
1 teaspoon cumin
3 tablespoons chopped cilantro
½ teaspoon red pepper flakes, or to taste
2 tablespoons fresh lemon juice, or to taste
2 tablespoons light olive oil

In a medium bowl, mix all ingredients. Cover and set aside; do not refrigerate.

1 1/2 cups

Pete's Barbecued Oysters

Pete Augusztiny, one of the owners of Wescott Bay Sea Farms on San Juan Island, provided this recipe, which can be served as an appetizer or entree. Westcott Bay grows two types of oysters, the common Pacific Oyster, and the rare European flat oyster. Apart from supplying many island restaurants, they ship gourmet oysters and clams worldwide. Island visitors can buy them on site.

> 20 Wescott Bay #1 oysters in the shell, washed
> ¼ pound butter
> 4 cloves garlic, minced
> 1 tablespoon capers
> 1 tablespoon finely chopped Italian parsley
> ½ cup bread crumbs
> 1 cup freshly grated Parmesan or Romano cheese

1. Preheat grill or barbecue. In a small saucepan, melt butter and sauté garlic about 1 minute. Add capers and parsley; heat through. Cover and set aside.

2. Place oysters, cupped-side down, on grill about 4 inches from heat source. When liquid in oysters begins to "spatter" and top shells begin to lift, about 5 minutes, remove top shells and return oysters to grill.

3. Brush butter mixture liberally over oysters. Sprinkle with bread crumbs and top with cheese. Cover and cook for 5 minutes more. Serve immediately.

4 servings

Downriggers' Crab Cakes
With Aioli Sauce

These delicate cakes from Downriggers on the Waterfront in Friday Harbor are gastronomical delights. Enjoy a delicious meal while watching the boats and ferry activity around the marina.

AIOLI SAUCE (recipe follows)
4 cups crab meat (1 pound)
¼ cup mayonnaise
1 egg, beaten
½ cup Panko (Japanese breadcrumbs)
1 tablespoon flour
2½ teaspoons fresh lemon juice
¼ cup finely diced red onion
1 cup finely diced celery
½ teaspoon salt
¼ teaspoon freshly ground pepper
Panko, to bread cakes
Butter

1. Prepare Aioli Sauce, following directions.

2. In a colander drain crab, using your hands to squeeze excess moisture from crab meat; place in a large bowl. Add remaining 9 ingredients (mayonnaise through pepper); mix thoroughly.

3. Shape crab mixture into 12 balls, pressing balls tightly together. Flatten balls into patties, dip into Panko, coating evenly on both sides. (The cakes are so delicate, they tend to fall apart, but continue to press together.)

4. In a large frying pan, over medium heat, melt butter. Fry cakes until golden-brown on each side, about 5 to 6 minutes total.

5. Transfer cakes to a heated serving platter. Serve with Aioli Sauce.

12 crab cakes

AIOLI SAUCE

A tangy lemon-garlic mayonnaise that is delicious served with seafoods, vegetables and meats.

6 medium garlic cloves
3 egg yolks
¼ cup fresh lemon juice
½ teaspoon salt
1 cup extra-virgin olive oil

1. In a food processor or blender, puree garlic. Add egg yolks, lemon and salt; blend until smooth.

2. While the machine is running, slowly pour oil into mixture. Blend until mixture is thick. Cover and refrigerate until ready to use. Sauce will keep for 4 days.   1 1/2 cups

Dry-Curried Shrimp

Serve these fiery shrimp as an appetizer with a chutney or chili sauce dip.

2 pounds large shrimp, peeled (leaving the tails) and deveined
1 tablespoon minced fresh garlic
1 teaspoon ground cumin
½ teaspoon red pepper flakes
2 tablespoons curry powder
¼ cup canola oil
2 teaspoons fresh lemon juice
1 teaspoon salt
¼ cup chopped cilantro, garnish

1. Rinse shrimp and pat dry; place in a bowl and set aside.

2. In a small bowl, combine garlic and spices. Sprinkle over shrimp and toss to coat. Allow to marinate for 30 minutes.

3. In a wok, over medium-high, heat oil and sauté until shrimp are almost opaque. Add lemon juice and salt; sauté 1 minute more or until shrimp are cooked through. Remove from heat, garnish.   6-8 servings

Arabian Shrimp Pâté

Robert Wood, owner-chef of the Bay Cafe on Lopez Island, developed this pâté to serve on his Cardamom Cornmeal Waffles. Chef Wood recommends serving the pâté with lightly steamed carrots dressed with melted butter, brown sugar, ginger and cinnamon.

> 3 tablespoons butter, divided
> 1 pound fresh shrimp, peeled and deveined
> 2 lemons, juiced
> ½ cup fresh bread crumbs
> ¼ cup calamata olives, pitted
> ½ cup toasted pine nuts
> 2 tablespoons chopped fresh parsley
> 2 tablespoons capers, drained
> 2 cloves garlic, chopped
> ½ teaspoon ground ginger
> ½ teaspoon ground turmeric
> ½ teaspoon ground cumin
> 1 teaspoon ground chili powder
> Salt, to taste
> CARDAMOM CORNMEAL WAFFLES (see page 31)

1. In medium frying pan, over medium, heat 1 tablespoon butter and sauté shrimp until they begin to turn pink. Stir in lemon juice.

2. Transfer shrimp and juice to a food processor and add remaining butter and remaining ingredients. Using the chopping blade, process the mixture by pulsing until completely smooth.

3. Empty the mixture into a lightly oiled one-quart pâté tureen. Chill the pâté for 2 hours before serving.

4. To serve, run a knife around edge of the tureen and invert onto a serving platter.   12 servings

Cardamom Cornmeal Waffles

These unusual waffles are served as an appetizer or a light meal with Arabian Shrimp Pâté at Lopez Island's Bay Cafe. Chef Robert Wood suggests serving them accompanied with a bowl of calamata olives and sliced cucumbers.

1½ cups unbleached white flour
½ cup yellow cornmeal, fine grind
2 teaspoons ground cardamom
1 teaspoon baking powder
1 teaspoon sugar
½ cup quinoa, cooked and drained
½ cup finely chopped fresh chives
¼ cup buttermilk
2 tablespoons corn oil
6 eggs, beaten

1. In a large mixing bowl, combine flour, cornmeal, cardamom, baking powder and sugar. In another bowl, mix together remaining ingredients.

2. Preheat oven 200° and heat waffle iron. Add the wet ingredients to dry ingredients and mix well.

3. Brush waffle iron surfaces with vegetable oil and pour about 1/3 cup of batter to make waffle. Cook until waffle is lightly browned. Repeat procedure for each waffle.

4. Cut waffles into wedges and transfer to a baking sheet. Place in oven and bake until crisp about 20-30 minutes. (Waffles can be made several day in advance and stored in an air tight container. Before using, crisp waffles by baking for a few minutes at 250°.)

5. To serve, place waffles in a serving dish and accompany with the Arabian Shrimp Pate.   6 waffles

Smoked Salmon Cheesecake

This creamy, rich salmon cheesecake was developed by Chef Mark Iverson for his Courtyard Cafe and catering business in Mount Vernon. Crab can be substituted for the salmon.

2¼ pounds cream cheese, (4½ 8-ounce packages)
1 cup heavy cream
3 eggs
2 cups smoked salmon
⅓ cup Parmesan cheese
Dash white pepper
1 tablespoon olive oil
½ medium onion, chopped
½ red bell pepper, chopped
½ green bell pepper, chopped
½ tablespoon minced garlic
1-2 tablespoons plain breadcrumbs
TOPPING
    1 (8-ounce) package cream cheese
    ¼ cup heavy cream
    ¾ cup smoked salmon
French bread or crackers

1. Preheat oven to 350°. In a food processor, place first 6 ingredients (cream cheese through pepper). Pulse to blend.

2. In a medium frying pan, heat oil and lightly sauté remaining ingredients except bread crumbs. Remove from heat and add sautéed vegetables to cheese mixture in food processor; pulse to combine.

3. Lightly grease a springform pan with butter and then sprinkle with bread crumbs. Spread mixture into pan.

4. Place springform pan in a larger shallow pan and place in oven. Pour hot water into the shallow pan about 3/4-inch deep. Bake mixture for 1 hour and 40 minutes. Turn off heat and leave pan in oven for an additional hour and 40 minutes.

5. Remove cake from oven and place on wire rack to cool. Refrigerate at least 2 hours before serving.

6. Prepare topping: In a food processor, blend cream cheese and heavy cream.

7. Remove cooled cheesecake from springform pan and place on a serving plate. Spread with topping and cover with smoked salmon. Refrigerate, if desired. Serve with French bread rounds or crackers.

12-inch cheesecake

Sockeye Salmon Tartare

Voted best Anacortes chef, Bill Ray serves this Northwest delicacy at the Salmon Run Bistro, where it is presented with the traditional accompaniments of sliced onion and hard-boiled egg.

2 pounds very fresh sockeye fillets, skinned and boned
½ cup minced red onions
2 anchovy fillets, minced
2½ tablespoons capers, drained
¼ cup chopped fresh parsley
2½ teaspoons stone-ground mustard
1½ tablespoons extra-virgin olive oil
3 tablespoons fresh grated horseradish
2-3 dashes hot pepper sauce
Salt and freshly ground pepper, to taste
Toast points (toasted bread, cut diagonally into triangles) or crackers
4 eggs, hard boiled and sliced
1 large red onion, sliced
Capers, garnish

1. Cut salmon fillets into 1-inch cubes. Place all ingredients in a food processor and pulse until combined. Do not puree; the tartare should be somewhat chunky.

2. Mound tartare in the center of a serving dish and circle with toast points or crackers, egg and onion slices. Garnish with capers and serve.

6-8 servings

Calamari Neapolitan

Chef Roberto A. Carrieri, of Roberto's on Friday Harbor, created this recipe out of necessity. He left instructions with the prep chef to "plump" one pound of raisins, but the prep chef misread the instructions as "10 pounds." So what to do with all those raisins? Chef Carrieri developed this unusual calamari appetizer which has become a restaurant favorite.

> ½ pound cleaned squid, cut into 1-inch rings
> ½ cup flour
> ½ cup olive oil
> ½ cup toasted pine nuts
> ½ cup raisins, plumped
> ¼ cup chopped garlic
> ¾ cup chopped Roma tomatoes
> ¼ cup chopped fresh parsley
> 2 lemons, juiced
> Lemon wedges, garnish

1. Place squid on a plate and lightly dust with flour. In a large, non-reactive, frying pan, over high, heat oil. Sauté squid about 1 minute on one side; add pine nuts, raisins and garlic.

2. With a spatula, turn squid over and sauté for 1 minute; add tomatoes, parsley and lemon juice. Stir to combine ingredients and heat through.

3. Transfer to serving dish and garnish with lemon wedges.   8 servings

Bud's Pickled Herring

It has become a family tradition to have the first tasting of this festive appetizer on Christmas Eve. Pickled herring makes a special gift for friends. The best brined herring we have found can be bought at the Conway Grocery Store.

> 2 cups white sugar
> 2 cups white vinegar
> 1 cup water
> 2 pounds brined herring, boned and skinned
> 2 large white onions, sliced into rings
> ¼ cup pickling spice

1. Prepare pickling marinade: In a large stainless pot, combine first 3 ingredients. Over high heat, bring marinade to a boil. Stir until sugar is dissolved. Remove from heat and allow to cool in refrigerator.

2. Place herring in a colander and gently rinse. Cut herring into bite-size pieces. In a 1-gallon glass or non-corrosive container, alternate layers of herring, onion and pickling spice until jar is full.

3. Pour marinade to cover mixture. If there are remaining ingredients, repeat procedure in another jar.

4. Cover and refrigerate for at least 3 weeks. Left in the marinade, the pickled herring will keep up to a year in the refrigerator.   1 gallon

Porter's West Beach Salsa

Linda Porter of Guemes Island is a gracious and popular hostess who makes this colorful, piquant salsa. We were delighted she agreed to share her "secret recipe" with us.

5 medium tomatoes
1 large jalapeno chili pepper, chopped
5 limes, juiced
2 cups diced red bell peppers
2 cups diced yellow bell peppers
2 cups diced green bell peppers
4 cups diced Roma tomatoes
1 cup fresh cilantro, finely chopped
2 cups green onions, including tops, finely chopped
1½ tablespoons minced fresh garlic
2 teaspoons salt
1 tablespoon sugar

1. In a blender, puree tomatoes and jalapeno; pour into large bowl. (Pureed mixture should measure about 4 cups.)

2. Stir in remaining ingredients. For additional heat, add more jalapeno peppers, as desired. Cover and refrigerate overnight. Salsa will keep for a week. Serve with chips and enjoy.   2 1/2 quarts

Mango Salsa

Patty Johnson of Fidalgo Island, serves this colorful, wonderfully fruity salsa as an appetizer with tortilla chips or as an accompaniment to fresh grilled halibut, salmon or pork tenderloin. We first enjoyed it at Strawberry Bay on Cypress Island. Papaya can be substituted for the mango.

> 3 firm-ripe mangos, peeled and diced
> 4 ripe Roma tomatoes, seeded and diced
> 1 medium red onion, finely chopped
> ½ cup chopped fresh cilantro
> 2 to 4 jalapeno chili peppers, seeded and diced
> ½ teaspoon crushed red pepper flakes
> 1 lime, juiced

In a medium bowl, combine all ingredients. Cover and refrigerate for at least 1 hour before serving. 4 cups

Baked Balsamic Onions

Anne McCracken shared this sweet-flavored appetizer with us. The golden amber of the caramelized onion offers terrific eye appeal.

> 3 large onions, thinly sliced
> 2 tablespoons extra-virgin olive oil
> ¼ to ½ cup balsamic vinegar
> 2 rounded tablespoons chopped garlic
> 1 teaspoon salt
> ½ teaspoon pepper
> 1 baguette, thinly sliced

1. Preheat oven to 350°. In a large heavy-bottomed pot, combine all ingredients. Toss to coat onions.

2. Bake, uncovered, for 1 hour, stirring occasionally to prevent burning. Add more vinegar, if mixture appears dry. Continue cooking until onions caramelize, up to an additional hour. Stir as needed.

3. Serve hot on bread slices or our Bruschetta on page 19. 1 1/2 cups

Hummus

Serve this garlic-flavored puree made from garbanzo beans and tahini with our Parmesan Pita Triangles, Bruschetta or raw vegetables.

1 cup dried garbanzo beans
6 tablespoons fresh lemon juice
6 cloves garlic, minced
½ cup tahini* (sesame seed paste)
3 tablespoons extra-virgin olive oil
½ teaspoon red pepper (Tabasco) sauce
1 teaspoon cumin
1 teaspoon salt
Paprika, garnish
¼ cup chopped fresh parsley or cilantro, garnish
Extra-virgin olive oil, garnish

1. In a colander, rinse and sort dry beans. Place beans in a medium saucepan, add cold water to cover. Let soak overnight.

2. Drain beans and return to pan with enough fresh water to measure 2 inches above the beans. Bring to a boil, reduce heat to low and simmer, covered, 30 minutes. With lid ajar, continue simmering until the skins begin to crack and the beans are tender, about 30 minutes more. (Check for doneness from time to time.) Drain beans, reserving the cooking liquid.

3. In a food processor or blender, combine the cooked beans, lemon juice, minced garlic, tahini, olive oil, red pepper sauce, cumin, salt, plus 2 tablespoons of the reserved cooking liquid. Process until soft and creamy. Add more cooking liquid, if needed. Adjust seasonings to taste.

4. To serve, mound hummus on a serving plate and garnish with paprika. Sprinkle chopped parsley around outer edge of hummus. Drizzle with olive oil garnish. Serve with bread or as a dip for vegetables.

2 1/2 cups

Available in most grocery stores.

Peppered Hot Wings

For an appetizer or lunch, you can enjoy these spicy chicken wings at the Garden Cafe on Orcas Island. The sauce can be made ahead and kept in the freezer. It is also a great marinade for fish, pork, beef or tofu.

   1 cup soy sauce
   ¼ cup ketchup
   ¼ cup sucanat* (or sugar of choice)
   5-6 cloves garlic, minced
   1 tablespoon crushed red pepper flakes (or ¼ cup Kim Chee Chili Pepper*)
   ½ teaspoon cayenne pepper
   1 cup sesame oil
   1-1½ pounds chicken wings, tips removed and wings cut at joint

1. In a large bowl, combine all ingredients, except chicken. Add chicken and toss to coat; cover and refrigerate for at least 3 hours.

2. Preheat oven to 375°. Line a large baking sheet with foil and place wings in a single layer. Bake for 35-40 minutes. Serve hot or cold.

6 servings

Available at Asian or specialty food markets.

Caramelized Pecans

These nuts are delicious and habit forming. Other nuts such as walnuts or almonds can be used.

> 2 cups whole pecan halves
> Boiling water
> ½ cup sugar
> ¼ cup peanut or corn oil
> Salt to taste

1. Place the nuts in a large bowl, add enough boiling water to cover. Soak for about 5 minutes.

2. Drain the nuts and pour them into a medium bowl. Sprinkle with sugar, tossing the nuts until they are thoroughly coated with the sugar. It may be necessary to sprinkle nuts with additional water to make all the sugar cling and almost melt.

3. Arrange the nuts in a single layer on parchment paper and dry them overnight.

4. In a wok or small sauté pan, heat oil over medium-high heat. Fry the nuts until they are golden brown and caramelized, about 2 minutes. (Be careful not to burn.)

5. Remove browned nuts with a slotted spoon and place on a plate to cool; sprinkle lightly with salt.

6. Serve warm or at room temperature. They can be stored for up to 2 weeks in a tightly sealed container.   2 cups

Baked Brie with Chutney

This elegant and easy appetizer provides a surprising combination of flavors.

¼ cup chopped pecans
1 teaspoon curry powder
1 (8-ounce) wheel of Brie or Camembert, at room temperature
¼ cup chopped fruit chutney
Red grapes, garnish
Crackers or baguette slices

1. Preheat oven to 350°. Place pecans in a shallow baking pan and bake for about 7 minutes or until lightly toasted. Remove from oven and set aside.

2. Sprinkle curry over cheese and rub into top and sides. Press pecans into the top and sides of cheese. Place cheese in center of pie pan and top evenly with chutney.

3. Bake cheese for 10 minutes or soft and heated through. Transfer to a serving dish and garnish with grapes. Serve warm with crackers or bread.

4 servings

Cabbage Salsa

Marianne Mach and her sister Sally Knutson own The Dish Ran Away With The Spoon, an Anacortes store that features an eclectic blend of housewares and "cool stuff." Marianne has hosted cooking classes in her home for many years. She serves this salsa with chips or as an accompaniment to chicken that is seasoned with cumin and garlic, grilled, shredded and wrapped in corn tortillas.

> 1 head (10 cups) red or green cabbage, chopped
> 2 bunches cilantro, chopped
> 2 (10-ounce) cans Ro-Tel tomatoes with green chilies*
> 3 cloves garlic, minced
> ½ cup balsamic vinegar
> 5 to 6 Roma tomatoes, chopped (optional)
> 1 avocado, peeled and chopped (optional)
> Salt and freshly ground pepper, to taste

In a large bowl, combine all ingredients. Adjust seasonings to taste. Cover and chill at least 2 hours. 8 cups

Available in the Mexican food section of most food markets. If unavailable, substitute diced canned tomatoes and diced green chilies.

Salads

PETER D. CAPEN

English Camp, San Juan Island

Mixed Greens
With Blue Cheese and Glazed Pecans

This simple yet elegant salad is accented with the sharp flavor of blue cheese and the sweet crunch of pecans. The Glazed Pecans can be prepared ahead of time. Gorgonzola can be substituted for blue cheese.

GLAZED PECANS (recipe follows)
MUSTARD VINAIGRETTE (recipe follows)
6 cups mixed greens (red leaf, bibb lettuce), rinsed and dried
½ cup crumbled blue cheese

1. Prepare Glazed Pecans; set aside to cool.

2. Prepare Mustard Vinaigrette, cover and refrigerate.

3. Tear lettuce into bite-size pieces and place on individual salad plates.

4. With a sharp knife, coarsely chop pecans. Sprinkle blue cheese and pecans over greens.

5. Pour vinaigrette over salad and serve immediately.   6 servings

GLAZED PECANS
Serve the leftover pecans as an appetizer or to dress-up a dessert.

2 tablespoons corn syrup
1 tablespoon brown sugar
2 tablespoons butter
½ teaspoon salt
½ pound shelled pecan halves

1. Preheat oven to 325°. Line a baking sheet with foil.

2. In a medium saucepan, combine all ingredients except pecans. Over medium-high, stir constantly and heat until butter melts and sugar dissolves. Mix in pecans and stir to coat. Remove from heat.

3. Using a large spoon, remove pecans and spread in a single layer on prepared baking sheet. Bake for 20-30 minutes, stirring occasionally. (Be

careful not to burn.) Remove from oven and allow to cool on baking sheet. Stir to loosen from foil.

4. Store in covered container and refrigerate until needed.   2 1/2 cups

MUSTARD VINAIGRETTE

1 tablespoon Dijon mustard
⅓ cup balsamic vinegar
1 tablespoon finely chopped shallots or
    1 clove minced garlic
1 teaspoon sugar
½ teaspoon salt
Freshly ground pepper
⅔ cup extra-virgin olive oil

In a small bowl, combine all ingredients except oil. Add oil gradually, beating with a whisk until blended. Cover and refrigerate, if made ahead.

1 cup

Katrina's Garlic Blue Cheese Dressing

This versatile dressing was developed by Kate Stone of Katrina's Restaurant in Friday Harbor and is a favorite with her customers. She serves it over mixed greens or baked potatoes as a spread for sandwiches, or as a vegetable dip.

1 to 2 tablespoons minced fresh garlic
½ cup crumbled blue cheese or Gorgonzola cheese
1 cup mayonnaise
1 cup sour cream
⅓ cup milk
1 teaspoon cider vinegar
½ teaspoon Worcestershire Sauce

In a mixing bowl, combine all ingredients. Cover and refrigerate, if made ahead.   3 cups

Pear Salad with Gorgonzola

A perfect salad for fall, when pears are at their best. The toasted walnuts complement the crisp, fresh pears and the creamy, rich Gorgonzola.

¼ cup chopped walnuts
MUSTARD VINAIGRETTE (see page 46)
1 bunch red leaf lettuce
2 fresh chilled pears (Bartlett, Bosc, d'Anjou)
⅓ cup crumbled Gorgonzola cheese

1. Preheat oven to 350°. In a small oven-proof dish, toast walnuts for about 5 minutes. (Or toast in the microwave on high, about 2 minutes.) Set aside to cool.

2. Prepare Mustard Vinaigrette.

3. Tear lettuce into bite-size pieces and place on individual salad plates. Core and slice pears into thin wedges, lay on greens.

4. Sprinkle toasted walnuts and crumbled cheese over greens and pears. Pour vinaigrette over salad and serve.   4-6 servings

Spinach Salad with Beets, Chèvre And Toasted Walnut Vinaigrette

Laurie Paul and Tim Barrette are chefs at the Friday Harbor House on San Juan Island. In summer they serve a spinach salad with island strawberries, pine nuts, feta cheese and a simple balsamic vinaigrette. But in winter, they combine spinach with earthy beets, rich goat cheese and sweet toasted walnut vinaigrette to create this outstanding salad.

> 4 medium red or candy-striped beets
> TOASTED WALNUT VINAIGRETTE (recipe follows)
> ½ pound spinach, stemmed and washed
> 6 ounces Chèvre (goat cheese)*
> ½ cup toasted walnuts

1. Place beets in a saucepan and add enough cold water to cover. Heat to boiling and reduce heat. Cover pan and simmer beets until tender. Drain beets and rinse in cold water. Peel and cut each beet into eighths and set aside.

2. Prepare Toasted Walnut Vinaigrette; cover and refrigerate.

3. Tear spinach leaves into bite-size pieces and place on individual chilled plates. Divide beets evenly between plates and top with crumbled Chèvre and toasted walnuts.

4. Drizzle vinaigrette over salads and serve. Additional vinaigrette may be served at the table.

4 servings

Available in the cheese section of most food markets.

TOASTED WALNUT VINAIGRETTE

1 medium shallot, peeled and chopped
¼ cup toasted walnuts
1 tablespoon apple cider vinegar
1 tablespoon unseasoned rice vinegar
¼ cup seasoned rice vinegar
¾ teaspoon sugar
¼ teaspoon ground cinnamon
¼ cup walnut oil
½ cup plus 2 tablespoons (5 ounces) corn oil or untoasted sesame oil
1 to 2 tablespoons water

1. In a food processor, combine shallot and walnuts and pulse until the mixture forms a loose paste. Add vinegars, sugar and cinnamon; process until fairly smooth.

2. With the motor running, add oils in a thin stream to create a smooth mixture. Add water to thin to desired consistency. Cover and refrigerate, if made ahead.   1 1/4 cups

Spinach and Citrus Salad

We hope you enjoy this bright mix of textures and tastes.

ORANGE GINGER DRESSING (recipe follows)
1 bunch spinach, stemmed and washed
1 grapefruit
2 oranges
2 cups finely sliced red cabbage
½ red onion, thinly sliced
1 avocado, sliced

1. Prepare Ginger Dressing; cover and refrigerate.

2. Tear spinach into bite-size pieces and place in a large salad bowl.

3. With a very sharp paring knife, cut the tops and bottoms from the grapefruit and oranges, then cut away and discard the remaining peel and outer membrane.

4. Holding the fruit over a small bowl, cut out the sections of pulp, allowing them to fall into the bowl. There should be no membrane around fruit sections.

5. Place fruit, cabbage, onions and avocado on spinach. Pour dressing over salad and gently toss. Serve on individual chilled salad plates.

6 servings

ORANGE GINGER DRESSING

¼ cup freshly squeezed orange juice
1 to 2 teaspoons freshly grated ginger root
¼ cup red wine vinegar
1 tablespoon tamari or soy sauce
¼ teaspoon salt
⅛ teaspoon freshly ground pepper
½ cup vegetable oil

In a small bowl, combine all ingredients, except oil. Add oil gradually, beating with a whisk until blended. Cover and refrigerate, if made ahead.

1 1/3 cups

Greek Romaine Salad

Crisp romaine dresses up this traditional Mediterranean salad. The peperoncinis provide additional zest.

BALSAMIC VINAIGRETTE (recipe follows)
1 head romaine, rinsed, drained and chilled
2 medium tomatoes, cut into wedges
1 cucumber, seeded and sliced
½ medium red onion, thinly sliced into rings
½ red or green bell pepper, julienned
⅓ cup sliced calamata or ripe olives
½ cup crumbled Feta cheese
¼ cup peperoncinis (pickled chilies)*

1. Prepare Balsamic Vinaigrette; cover and refrigerate.

2. Tear romaine into bite-size pieces and place in a salad bowl. Add remaining ingredients.

3. Pour vinaigrette over salad and gently toss. Serve immediately.

6 servings

BALSAMIC VINAIGRETTE

⅓ cup balsamic vinegar
2 tablespoons fresh lemon juice
½ teaspoon dried basil
1 clove garlic, minced
½ teaspoon sugar
¼ teaspoon salt
¼ teaspoon freshly ground pepper
⅔ cup extra-virgin olive oil

In a small bowl, combine all ingredients, except oil. Add oil gradually, blending with a whisk. Cover and refrigerate, if made ahead.   1 cup

Available in the delicatessan section of most food markets.

Caesar Salad with Parmesan Croutons

This salad is still one of our all-time favorites. In our opinion, a true Caesar must contain anchovy fillets. Homemade croutons accent this classic salad.

1 cup PARMESAN CROUTONS (recipe follows)
1 large head romaine, washed
1 egg
3 tablespoons fresh lemon juice
1 teaspoon Dijon mustard
1 clove garlic, minced
⅓ cup extra-virgin olive oil
6 anchovy fillets, rinsed and chopped
Freshly ground black pepper, to taste
⅓ cup freshly grated Parmesan cheese

1. Prepare Parmesan Croutons.

2. Tear romaine into bite-size pieces, place in a plastic bag and refrigerate until needed.

3. Coddle egg: Fill a small saucepan half-full of water and bring to a boil. Place egg on a spoon and carefully lower it into the boiling water. Remove pan from heat and let egg stand in water for 1 minute. Remove egg and place in a bowl of cold water. Set aside.

4. Prepare dressing: In a small bowl, mix lemon juice, mustard and garlic. Add oil gradually, beating with a whisk until blended. Add anchovies and set aside.

5. Place chilled romaine in a large salad bowl. Grind pepper over romaine. Pour dressing over salad and toss gently to coat greens. Break coddled egg into salad, toss again. Sprinkle with cheese and croutons and toss before serving.   4-6 servings

PARMESAN CROUTONS
Croutons can be made a day or two ahead of time and refrigerated.

> 6 slices bread
> 2 tablespoons butter or margarine
> 2 tablespoons extra-virgin olive oil
> 1 clove garlic, minced
> ¼ cup finely grated Parmesan cheese
> ¼ teaspoon paprika

1. Preheat oven to 300°. Using a serrated knife, cut crusts from bread. Cut bread into 1/2-inch cubes.

2. In a large frying pan, over medium, heat butter and olive oil. Add minced garlic and bread cubes; stir until covered with butter mixture. Sprinkle with Parmesan cheese and paprika.

3. Transfer bread cubes to a baking sheet and spread in a single layer. Bake until crisp and lightly browned, about 25-30 minutes.

4. Remove from oven and allow to cool. Croutons can be stored for up to 2 days in an airtight container.

2 cups

Chicken Caesar Salad

Chimayo Restaurant in Eastsound on Orcas Island serves this flavorful salad with warm handmade tortillas and salsa. It is equally good served with tortilla chips, or crusty bread.

CREAMY SERRANO DRESSING (recipe follows)
GARLIC-CHILI CROUTONS (recipe follows)
2 heads romaine, rinsed and chilled
½ head shredded red cabbage
1 pound skinned and boned chicken breasts, cooked
1 bunch green onions, chopped
½ cup freshly grated Parmesan cheese
½ cup chopped fresh cilantro
8 lime wedges

1. Prepare Creamy Serrano Dressing; cover and refrigerate. Prepare Garlic-Chili Croutons; cover and set aside.

2. Tear romaine into bite-size pieces and place in a large salad bowl. Add red cabbage and cooked chicken. Toss salad with enough dressing to coat. Transfer salad to individual salad plates.

3. Garnish each salad with green onions, Parmesan, cilantro, Garlic-Chili Croutons and a lime wedge.   8-10 servings

CREAMY SERRANO DRESSING

½ cup freshly squeezed lime juice
1 tablespoon Dijon mustard
2 tablespoons chopped fresh serrano or jalapeno chili pepper
3 egg yolks or ¾ cup plain yogurt
2 tablespoons freshly chopped garlic
½ teaspoon salt
1½ teaspoons pepper
2 cups canola oil

In a food processor, combine all ingredients except oil. Add oil gradually, through feed tube with machine running. Cover and refrigerate, if made ahead.   3 cups

GARLIC-CHILI CROUTONS

½ loaf sourdough bread, cut into ½-inch cubes
2 tablespoons freshly chopped garlic
Dash of cayenne
Dash of chili powder
½ teaspoon salt
⅛ teaspoon pepper
¼ cup canola oil

1. Preheat oven to 400°. In a medium bowl, combine all ingredients and toss to coat evenly.

2. Spread croutons on a baking sheet and bake for 10 to 15 minutes until golden and crunchy.

3. Remove from oven and set aside to cool. Store in a covered container, if made ahead.   3-4 cups

Tomato and Bread Salad

For this bread salad, we use a coarse-grained bread from La Vie en Rose Bakery in Anacortes. This is one of those salads that makes you want to pack a picnic basket with some cheese and a bottle of red wine and take off for a day on the beach.

1½ pounds Roma tomatoes, seeded and coarsely chopped (about 2 ½ cups)
½ English cucumber, seeded and chopped
½ cup chopped green bell pepper
1 (15-ounce) can garbanzo beans, drained and rinsed
½ red onion, chopped
½ cup chopped fresh parsley
¼ cup chopped fresh basil
1 cup sliced green olives (optional)
3 tablespoons red wine vinegar
1½ tablespoons extra-virgin olive oil
1 clove garlic, minced
¼ teaspoon salt
¼ teaspoon coarsely ground pepper
4 cups coarse-grained bread cubes (½-inch)

1. In a large bowl, combine first 8 ingredients (tomatoes through olives). Sprinkle next 5 ingredients (vinegar through pepper) over tomato mixture and toss to blend. Cover and set aside to marinate. Mixture can be refrigerated at this time.

2. Preheat oven to 300°. Arrange bread cubes in a single layer on baking sheet. Bake in oven, stirring frequently, until toasted, about 15 minutes. Set aside to cool.

3. Thirty minutes before serving, combine bread cubes with marinated tomato mixture. Serve at room temperature.   4-6 servings

Shaw Island Salad with Tahini Dressing

This unusual dressing gives a unique flavor to a simple salad.

> TAHINI DRESSING (recipe follows)
> 6 cups mixed salad greens, rinsed and dried
> 1½ cups grated carrots
> 1 cup finely sliced red cabbage
> 1 cucumber, skinned and sliced
> ¼ cup sunflower seeds
> 1 cup alfalfa sprouts

1. Prepare Tahini Dressing.

2. In a large salad bowl, combine all salad ingredients except sprouts. Pour dressing over salad and toss gently.

3. Place salad on individual chilled salad plates and top with sprouts. Serve immediately.
6 servings

TAHINI DRESSING

> 1 clove garlic, minced
> ½ cup tahini (sesame paste)
> ½ cup fresh lemon juice
> 1 tablespoon soy sauce
> ¼ cup olive oil
> ¼ cup water

1. In a mixing bowl, combine all ingredients except water. Beat in water gradually until the dressing is the consistency of heavy cream. Adjust seasoning, to taste.

2. Serve immediately or cover and refrigerate for up to 4 days. Return to room temperature before using and mix well.
1 1/2 cups

Black Bean and Corn Salad

You will enjoy the lively flavors of the Southwest in this colorful, robust salad.

2 (15-ounce) cans black beans, drained and rinsed
1½ cups corn kernels, fresh or thawed
1 large red bell pepper, diced
1 cup chopped celery
¾ cup minced red onion
2 fresh jalapeno chili peppers, seeded and minced
½ cup chopped fresh cilantro
2 teaspoons cumin seed
LIME DRESSING
    ¼ cup lime juice
    ½ tablespoon lime zest
    2 tablespoons brown sugar
    1 tablespoon Dijon mustard
    ½ teaspoon red pepper flakes
    ½ teaspoon salt
    Freshly ground pepper, to taste
    ¼ cup vegetable oil
Cilantro sprigs, garnish

1. In a large bowl, combine all salad ingredients and set aside.

2. In a small bowl, combine all dressing ingredients, except oil. Add oil gradually, beating with a whisk until blended.

3. Pour dressing over salad and toss to combine. Cover and refrigerate for at least one hour. Salad can be served cold or at room temperature. Garnish with cilantro sprigs before serving.　　　　　6-8 servings

Summer Island Ceviche

Ceviche requires the freshest seafood available, since it is "cooked" only in lime juice and vinegar. The islands of Puget Sound are one of the last Northwest places where small fleets market their catch daily. Enjoy this refreshing seafood dish at Christina's Restaurant in Eastsound, on Orcas Island.

    1 cup fresh lime juice
    ½ cup seasoned rice wine vinegar
    2-4 cloves garlic, mashed
    1 red onion, slivered
    1 pound fresh scallops
    1 pound fresh halibut, cut into 1-inch cubes
    1 sweet red pepper, cut into ½-inch dice
    1 small cucumber, peeled and seeded, cut into ½-inch cubes
    1 small papaya, peeled and seeded, cut into ½-inch cubes
    4 tablespoons minced fresh cilantro
    2 tablespoons minced fresh lemon balm or mint
    1 head butter lettuce, washed and chilled
    1 fresh lime, cut into 6 wedges, garnish

1. In a large glass, ceramic or plastic bowl, combine lime juice, vinegar, garlic and onion. Add seafood and toss lightly to coat. Cover and marinate in the refrigerator for 4 hours or overnight.

2. One half-hour before serving, add the red peppers, cucumber, papaya, cilantro and mint.

3. Serve Ceviche on leaves of butter lettuce and garnish with lime wedges.

6 servings

Shrimp Stuffed Avocado
With Sun-Dried Tomato Vinaigrette

Chef Bill Ray owns Salmon Run Bistro in Anacortes' beautifully restored Majestic Hotel. His culinary expertise and sense of adventure have led him to chef positions in locations as diverse as Carmel, Monterey, Maui and Friday Harbor on San Juan Island.

SUN-DRIED TOMATO VINAIGRETTE (recipe follows)
8 slices bacon, diced
1 pound bay shrimp
1 tablespoon fresh lemon juice
½ cup mayonnaise
½ cup diced celery
¼ cup chopped green onion
½ teaspoon chopped fresh garlic
¼ cup diced green bell pepper
¼ cup diced red bell pepper
1 tablespoon chopped fresh parsley
Salt and freshly ground pepper, to taste
1 bunch baby lettuce, rinsed and dried
2 ripe avocados, halved, peeled and stoned
1 cucumber, julienned
1 carrot, julienned
1 stalk celery, julienned
1 small red onion, sliced
6 radishes, sliced or cut into roses
Assorted edible flowers, garnish

1. Prepare Sun-Dried Tomato Vinaigrette; cover and refrigerate for at least 2 hours. In a small frying pan, cook bacon until crisp. Remove from pan and drain on paper towels; set aside.

2. In a medium bowl, gently combine next ten ingredients (shrimp through salt and pepper) and set aside.

3. Divide lettuce evenly between 4 chilled plates and top each with an avocado half. Fill each avocado evenly with the shrimp mixture.

4. Arrange remaining vegetables around the perimeter of each plate in a decorative fashion. Sprinkle with bacon and garnish each plate with several flowers. Drizzle vinaigrette over salad and serve.   4 servings

SUN-DRIED TOMATO VINAIGRETTE

⅓ cup sun-dried tomatoes, julienned
½ cup balsamic vinegar
5 tablespoons fresh lemon juice
¼ cup chopped fresh basil
1½ teaspoons chopped fresh garlic
1½ teaspoons chopped fresh parsley
½ teaspoon salt
¼ teaspoon freshly ground pepper
1 cup extra-virgin olive oil

In a small bowl, combine all ingredients, except oil. Add oil gradually, beating with a whisk until blended. Cover and refrigerate for at least 2 hours.

2 cups

Picnic Coleslaw

Serve this traditional creamy salad at a beach picnic or backyard barbecue.

8 cups chopped cabbage
2 carrots, shredded
¼ cup sugar
¼ cup milk or buttermilk
1 cup mayonnaise
3 tablespoons cider vinegar
1 ½ teaspoons dried dill weed
1 teaspoon salt
⅛ teaspoon pepper

1. In a large bowl, combine cabbage and carrots and set aside.
2. In a small bowl, combine remaining ingredients and adjust seasonings to taste. Pour over cabbage mixture and toss to coat. Cover and refrigerate for at least 1 hour. Stir before serving.   4-6 servings

Big Lee's Cabbage Salad

After a day of motorcycling in the islands, Big Lee hosts his friends on the beach with barbecued salmon and this crisp and crunchy salad. Chicken, shrimp or crab can be added to make a main dish.

ASIAN DRESSING (recipe follows)
3 tablespoons vegetable oil or butter
2 (3-ounce) packages ramen noodles, broken
½ cup sliced almonds
8 cups cabbage, diced
½ cup sliced green onions
⅓ cup toasted sesame seeds

1. Prepare Asian Dressing and set aside.

2. In a large frying pan, over medium, heat oil and sauté noodles and almonds until lightly toasted. Remove from heat and allow to cool.

3. In a large bowl, combine cabbage and onions; mix in sautéed noodles and almonds. Add sesame seeds.

4. Toss salad with dressing. Cover and refrigerate at least one hour before serving.

8-10 servings

ASIAN DRESSING

⅓ - ½ cup sugar
¼ cup white or rice vinegar
1 tablespoon soy sauce
2 teaspoons sesame oil
½ cup vegetable oil

In a medium bowl, combine all ingredients except vegetable oil. Add oil gradually, blending with a whisk. Cover and refrigerate, if made ahead.

3/4 cup

Art's Potato Salad

Creamy potatoes are laced with garlic in this summertime favorite. It's a perfect dish to take to a beach potluck.

8 medium new potatoes
4 eggs, hard-boiled and chopped
1 cup sliced radishes
½ cup finely chopped red onion
3 cloves garlic, minced
½ cup chopped dill pickles
¾ cup chopped green olives
1 cup mayonnaise
3 tablespoons Dijon mustard
2 teaspoons red wine vinegar
1 teaspoon dried dill weed
Salt and freshly ground pepper, to taste

1. Wash potatoes and cut in half. In a large pot, cook potatoes in boiling salted water until tender, about 20 minutes. Drain the potatoes and place in a large bowl.

2. Mash potatoes with a potato masher, leaving some chunks for texture. Stir in remaining ingredients.

3. Transfer to serving bowl, cover and refrigerate for at least 2 hours.

6-8 servings

Gorgonzola Potato Salad

Proprietor and Chef Michael Magerkurth of Geppetto's, in Anacortes on Fidalgo Island, offers fine catering as well as gourmet Italian specialties, fresh pastas and homemade sauces. Michael uses a special smoker for the potatoes in this salad. However, since most of us do not have one, we have chosen to roast them. If you want the smoky flavor, barbecuing is necessary.

> 2½ pounds baby red potatoes, washed
> 1½ cups chopped green onions
> ½ cup cooked chopped bacon
> 8 ounces Gorgonzola cheese, crumbled
> 1 cup sour cream
> 1 cup mayonnaise
> 8 ounces basil pesto

1. Preheat oven to 375°. Place potatoes on oven rack and roast for 20 minutes, or until tender when pierced with a fork. Remove from oven and allow to cool. Cut potatoes into quarters and place in a large bowl.

2. In a medium bowl, combine remaining ingredients. Add to potatoes and mix gently. Cover and refrigerate for at least 2 hours.   6-8 servings

Confetti Rice Salad

Sandy Warmouth of North Beach brought this to a community potluck, where it was a hit with everyone. It is best to serve this salad the day it is made, but it will keep one to two days, refrigerated.

DIJON VINAIGRETTE (recipe follows)
2 cups uncooked long-grain rice
4 cups chicken stock
¼ cup chopped green onion, including some tops
¼ cup finely chopped sun-dried tomatoes
½ cup sliced black olives
1 cup chopped red bell pepper
1 cup chopped green bell pepper
1 medium carrot, julienned
1 (6-ounce) jar marinated artichoke hearts, drained and sliced
Salt and freshly ground pepper, to taste

1. Prepare Dijon Vinaigrette; cover and set aside.

2. In a medium pan, cook rice in chicken stock according to package instructions. Remove from heat. For fluffier rice, place paper towel over top of pan, cover with lid and let rest for 5 minutes.

3. Transfer rice to a large bowl.

4. Whisk vinaigrette well; add to warm rice and toss.

5. Gently stir in remaining ingredients; season with salt and pepper to taste. Cover and refrigerate for at least 2 hours before serving.   6-8 servings

DIJON VINAIGRETTE
Make ahead, if possible, to give the flavors time to meld.

¼ cup rice vinegar
¼ cup white vinegar
¼ teaspoon sugar
1 tablespoon Dijon mustard
¼ cup chopped fresh basil or 1 teaspoon dried
1 tablespoon chopped fresh oregano or ½ teaspoon dried
Salt and freshly ground pepper, to taste

½ cup extra-virgin olive oil

In a bowl, combine all ingredients except oil. Add oil gradually, beating with a whisk until blended. Cover and refrigerate.   1 cup

Gallette Salad

This rustic peasant bread salad is a favorite with Dawn's family. Gallete are Italian hardtack biscuits, which provide the "bread" of the recipe. (Toasted coarse-grained bread may be subsituted for the Gallette, but it is worth trying to find the authentic ingredient.) The original recipe calls for sardines, which we have replaced with Dungeness crab to give a fresh Northwest flavor.

    3 Gallette biscuits*
    3 cups water
    1 cup cider vinegar
    6 hard-boiled eggs, coarsely chopped
    8 green onions with tops, coarsely chopped
    2 cups crab meat
    1½ cups mayonnnaise
    ½ teaspoon salt
    1 teaspoon freshly ground pepper

1. Break up Gallette into small chunks and place in a large bowl. Cover with water and vinegar for about 30 minutes, letting biscuits absorb the liquid. Using your fingers, crumble biscuits into small bite-size pieces.

2. Using hands, remove biscuits from vinegar solution and gently squeeze out excess liquid. Do not squeeze dry; biscuits should remain moist. About 1 cup of liquid will remain in the bowl; discard liquid. Transfer biscuits to large mixing bowl.

3. Stir in remaining ingredients to moistened biscuits and blend well. Cover and refrigerate for at least 6 hours before serving.   8 servings

Rice and Spinach Salad

Todd Wood, chef at the "Deli Next Door" at the Skagit Valley Food Co-op in Mt. Vernon, agreed to share this recipe with us. It is our favorite salad from the Deli. The complex flavors are a combination we hope you will enjoy as well.

> HERB VINAIGRETTE (recipe follows)
> 3 cups cooked brown rice, cooled
> ½ bunch fresh spinach, stemmed, washed and chopped
> 1 small red onion, finely chopped
> ½ pound feta cheese, crumbled
> ¼-½ cup chopped pecans
> ½ cup sliced black olives
> ½ red bell pepper, diced

1. Prepare Herb Vinaigrette; cover and refrigerate.
2. Place cooked rice in a large bowl and add remaining ingredients.
3. Pour 1/4 to 1/2 cup Herb Vinaigrette over salad and gently toss. Cover and refrigerate for at least 1 hour before serving.   4 servings

HERB VINAIGRETTE

Make ahead, if possible, to give the flavors time to meld. This vinaigrette keeps well in the refrigerator and can be used for other salads.

> ⅓ cup balsamic vinegar
> ½ teaspoon chopped fresh garlic
> ½ teaspoon each dried oregano, basil, marjoram
> ⅛ teaspoon ground fennel seed
> ¼ teaspoon salt
> ⅛ teaspoon freshly ground pepper
> ¼ cup extra-virgin olive oil
> ¾ cup canola oil

In a bowl, combine all ingredients, except oil. Add oil gradually, beating with a whisk until blended. Cover and refrigerate.   1 1/3 cups

Mango Chutney Pasta Salad

For people from all walks of life, Gere-a-Deli is one of the most popular noon-time gathering places in Anacortes. Laurie Gere has been serving up her special brand of hospitality since 1981. Her specialties are salads, generous sandwiches and scrumptious desserts.

1 (16-ounce) package penne pasta
3 cups bite-size broccoli florets
6 boned and skinned chicken breast halves, cooked
1 large red bell pepper, julienned
2 cups mayonnaise
2 cups mango chutney*
2 tablespoons mild curry powder
2-3 tablespoons honey
Salt and pepper, to taste

1. In a large pot, cook pasta al dente, according to package directions. Drain and rinse with cold water. Return to pot and set aside to cool.

2. In a medium saucepan, steam broccoli for 3 minutes, or until tender-crisp and bright green. Do not overcook. Drain and rinse with cold water, set aside.

3. Cut chicken into bite-sized pieces and place in large bowl. Add broccoli, red pepper and cooled pasta.

4. In a separate bowl, blend mayonnaise, chutney, curry and honey. Add to chicken mixture and gently toss to coat. Season with salt and pepper.

5. Cover and chill at least 2 hours before serving.   8 servings

*Available in most grocery stores.

Asian Pasta Salad

Proprietor and Chef Kate Stone of Katrina's Restaurant in Friday Harbor on San Juan Island creates innovative dishes amid the hustle and bustle of her kitchen. We enjoyed this salad, which can be adapted to feature seasonal vegetables.

GINGER SESAME DRESSING (recipe follows)
1 (8-ounce) package Chinese egg noodles or linguini
½ pound snow peas (asparagus or broccoli)
1½ cups sliced carrots
1 red bell pepper, julienned
2½ cups shredded green cabbage
1 bunch green onions, sliced diagonally
¼ cup chopped fresh cilantro (optional)
1 (8-ounce) can water chestnuts, drained and halved
1 (6-ounce) can baby corn, drained
Cashews, garnish

1. Prepare Ginger Sesame Dressing; cover and refrigerate.

2. Blanch snow peas: Place snow peas (asparagus or broccoli) in a large shallow bowl with 1/2-inch of water and cover tightly with plastic wrap. Microwave on high for a minute or two, drain and rinse with cold water. Blot dry with a paper towel and set aside.

3. In a large pot, cook pasta al dente, according to package directions. Drain and rinse with cold water. Place in large bowl, add dressing and toss to coat.

4. Gently fold in blanched vegetable and remaining ingredients. Cover and refrigerate for at least two hours.

5. To serve, place on individual plates and garnish with cashews.

6 servings

GINGER SESAME DRESSING
½ cup rice vinegar
¼ cup Tamari or soy sauce
3 tablespoons grated fresh ginger
¾ teaspoon red pepper flakes
3 tablespoons black sesame seeds* or
    toasted sesame seeds
¼ cup sesame oil

In a small bowl, combine all ingredients, except oil. Add oil gradually, beating with a whisk until blended. Cover and refrigerate, if made ahead.

1 cup

Available in health food stores.

Smoked Salmon Pasta Salad

Another great salad recipe from Todd Wood at the Skagit Valley Food Co-op. Serve this salad as a lunch or light summer evening meal.

HERB VINAIGRETTE (see page 68)
2 cups uncooked shell-shaped pasta (4 cups cooked)
¼ pound smoked salmon, skinned and cubed
½ red bell pepper, diced
1 small red onion, finely chopped
¼ cup chopped fresh parsley
½ cup frozen peas, thawed
1 small zucchini, quartered and sliced
1 cup freshly grated Parmesan cheese
2 teaspoons paprika

1. Prepare Herb Vinaigrette; cover and refrigerate.

2. In a large pot, cook pasta al dente, according to package directions. Drain, rinse with cold water.

3. Place cooled pasta in a large bowl, toss with 3/4 cup Herb Vinaigrette. Gently mix in remaining ingredients.

4. Cover and refrigerate for at least 1 hour. Add more vinaigrette as needed before serving.

4 servings

Mediterranean Pasta Salad

Some of the best ingredients from the Mediterranean region are highlighted in this colorful salad. For a more robust flavor, add green olives and anchovies.

    2 cups uncooked shell-shaped pasta
    1 cup BALSAMIC VINAIGRETTE (see page 51)
    ½ cup chopped celery
    ¼ cup chopped green onions, including some tops
    1 tablespoon capers
    1 (6-ounce) jar marinated artichoke hearts, drained and sliced
    2 tablespoons chopped fresh Italian parsley
    1 teaspoon dried oregano
    Salt and freshly ground pepper, to taste
    2 Roma tomatoes, chopped
    1 cup crumbled Feta cheese
    Italian parsley sprigs, garnish

1. In a large pot, cook pasta al dente, according to package directions. Drain and rinse with cold water.

2. While pasta is cooking, prepare Balsamic Vinaigrette. Transfer pasta to a large bowl and toss with vinaigrette. Stir in remaining ingredients, except tomatoes and cheese. Cover and refrigerate at least 2 hours.

3. Before serving, gently stir in tomatoes and cheese. Garnish with parsley sprigs and serve.   4 servings

Ginger Soba Noodle Salad

This recipe by Yuriko Bullock is a "hot" item at the Garden Cafe on Orcas. She serves it on a bed of mixed salad greens.

> 12 ounces Buckwheat noodles*
> 1 tablespoon canola oil
> 2 cups broccoli florets
> ¼ cup soy sauce
> 1 tablespoon Wasabi paste* (Japanese horseradish)
> 1½ tablespoons finely chopped ginger root
> 2 tablespoons toasted sesame seeds
> 1 tablespoon sucanat* (or sugar of choice)
> 2 tablespoons sesame oil
> ⅔ cup chopped green onions (with tops)
> 1 small red onion, thinly sliced
> 4 cups mixed greens (Bibb, red leaf, endive, escarole)

1. In a large pot, cook noodles *al dente*, according to package directions. Drain and rinse with cold water. Return to pot, add 1 tablespoon canola oil and toss to coat noodles. Set aside to cool.

2. In a medium saucepan, steam broccoli for 3 minutes, or until bright green and tender-crisp. Drain and rinse with cold water; add to noodles.

3. In a small bowl, combine soy sauce, Wasabi paste, ginger, sesame seeds and sweetener. Add oil, beating with a whisk until blended. Stir in green onions.

4. Pour prepared dressing over noodles and broccoli; gently toss to coat. (Noodle mixture can be refrigerated at this time.)

5. Arrange greens on individual salad plates. Top with noodle mixture and serve.

4-6 servings

Available at Asian or specialty food markets.

Wild Rice Hazelnut Salad

This nutty salad is a delicious wintertime accompaniment for a holiday dinner.

1½ cups wild rice
1 teaspoon salt
1 cup dried currants
1 cup hazelnuts
CITRUS-HAZELNUT VINAIGRETTE (recipe follows)
2 apples, diced
Salt and freshly ground pepper, to taste

1. Place rice in a large bowl with enough warm water to cover. Soak for 15 minutes and drain.

2. In a medium saucepan, bring 6 cups water and salt to a boil. Stir in rice and reduce heat. Cover and simmer until the rice is tender but still chewy, about 35-45 minutes. Remove pan from heat and drain rice in a colander. Transfer rice to a large bowl.

3. While rice is cooking, plump currants by placing them in a bowl and cover with boiling water; set aside. Preheat oven to 350°.

4. Place hazelnuts in a single layer in a shallow pan; toast in the oven about 7 minutes. Remove from oven and allow to cool a few minutes. Rub nuts with a towel to remove most of the skins. Coarsely chop nuts and set aside.

5. Prepare Citrus-Hazelnut Vinaigrette and set aside.

6. Drain currents and pat dry. Add currants to rice; pour in vinaigrette and toss to coat. Refrigerate at least 2 hours.

7. Before serving, stir in apples and hazelnuts. Salt and pepper, to taste.

6-8 servings

CITRUS-HAZELNUT VINAIGRETTE

2 tablespoons minced shallots
1 tablespoon fresh orange zest
½ cup orange juice
2 tablespoons lemon juice
1½ tablespoons balsamic vinegar
1 teaspoon salt
½ teaspoon fennel seeds, crushed
2 tablespoons hazelnut oil
⅔ cup extra-virgin olive oil

In a small bowl, combine all ingredients, except oils. Add oils gradually, blending with a whisk. Cover and refrigerate, if made ahead.   1 1/2 cups

Chop Chop Salad

This delicious chef salad provides an interesting combination of textures and flavors.

CREAMY VINAIGRETTE (recipe follows)
4 plum tomatoes, seeded and finely chopped
½ cup chopped red or green bell pepper
½ cup thinly sliced green onions
1 cup diced wine Italian salami
1 cup diced smoked turkey breast
1 cup diced Provolone cheese
1 cup canned garbanzo beans, drained
1 head romaine lettuce, finely chopped
Salt and freshly ground pepper, to taste

1. Prepare Creamy Vinaigrette and set aside.

2. In a large bowl, combine all salad ingredients except romaine. Add all vinaigrette and toss to coat. Ingredients can be refrigerated at this time.

3. Before serving, add romaine and toss. Salt and pepper to taste. Serve immediately. 6-8 servings

CREAMY VINAIGRETTE
½ cup mayonnaise
⅓ cup balsamic vinegar
2 tablespoons fresh lemon juice
1 tablespoon Dijon mustard
1 clove garlic, minced
2 teaspoons dried oregano
½ teaspoon salt
1 teaspoon freshly ground pepper
½ cup extra-virgin olive oil

In a small bowl, combine all ingredients, except oil. Add oil gradually, blending with a whisk. Cover and refrigerate, if made ahead. 1-3/4 cups

Entrees

MATT BROWN

Island Interior

Roasted Chicken
With Rosemary and Garlic

Fragrant aromas of garlic and rosemary will permeate the air and draw guests into the kitchen. This beautiful golden chicken will become the focal point for an elegant dinner.

1 (4-pound) roasting chicken
2 sprigs fresh rosemary (1 tablespoon dried)
4 cloves garlic, unpeeled and crushed
Salt and freshly ground pepper
1 tablespoon extra-virgin olive oil
Fresh rosemary sprigs, garnish

1. Preheat oven to 450°. Rinse the chicken and pat dry.

2. Place rosemary and garlic in the cavity of the chicken and sprinkle cavity with salt and pepper.

3. Rub oil over chicken skin and sprinkle with salt and pepper and place chicken on a rack in a roasting pan. Bake chicken about 25 minutes.

4. Reduce heat to 375° and and brush chicken with pan juices. Continue baking for 30 to 35 minutes more, or until golden brown and juices run clear when pierced with a fork.

5. Remove from oven, cover with foil and allow to rest for 10 minutes. Slice chicken and serve on a heated platter, garnished with rosemary sprigs.

4 servings

Hunter Chicken

Fidalgo Island resident Sharron Prosser serves this braised chicken with a robust tomato sauce over her recipe for Bistro Potatoes. It will surely become a favorite, elegant winter meal.

1 cup unbleached all-purpose flour
4 chicken hindquarters (thighs and legs together), washed and dried
¼ cup olive oil
1 medium onion, minced
3 ounces sliced pancetta or proscuitto, chopped (*available in the deli meat section*)
3 cloves garlic, minced
2 tablespoons finely chopped fresh rosemary or 1 tablespoon dried
1 cup Marsala wine
1 (28-ounce) can Italian tomatoes, with juice
Salt and freshly ground pepper, to taste
Bistro Potatoes, see page 185
½ cup chopped Italian parsley, garnish

1. Put flour in a plastic bag; add chicken and shake to coat.

2. In a large frying pan, heat oil over medium-high. Add chicken, making sure not to crowd the skillet. (Chicken can be browned in two batches.) Cook until golden brown on all sides, about 8 to 10 minutes. Remove chicken and set aside.

3. Reduce heat to medium, add onion, pancetta, garlic and rosemary. Sauté about 5 minutes until onion is golden.

4. Return chicken to pan, add Marsala and increase temperature to high. Cook until Marsala is almost reduced, 5 to 6 minutes. Add tomatoes and season with salt and pepper. Bring tomatoes to a boil and reduce heat to medium-low. Cover pan, with lid slightly ajar.

5. Cook until chicken is tender, 40 to 50 minutes. Turn chicken a few times during cooking. Adjust seasoning to taste.

6. While chicken is cooking prepare Bistro Potatoes.

7. Place potatoes on heated individual plates. Make a well in the center of the potatoes and place the chicken in the well. Spoon sauce over chicken and liberally garnish with parsley.   4 servings

Tuscan Chicken with Garbanzo Beans

This easy to make, peasant dish will delight guests as well as your family. The creamy garbanzos offer a pleasant change from the usual pasta or rice.

2 skinned chicken breasts (4 breast halves)
½ cup flour
3 tablespoons extra-virgin olive oil
Salt and freshly ground pepper
1 medium onion, chopped
2 large cloves garlic, minced
¾ cup dry red wine
1 (14½-ounce) can diced tomatoes in juice, do not drain
2 (15½-ounce) cans garbanzo beans, drained
½ cup sliced ripe olives
½ cup chopped fresh Italian parsley
½-1 teaspoon ground cinnamon
2 teaspoons dried thyme
Salt and pepper, to taste

1. Cut each breast in half. Put flour in plastic bag; add chicken and shake to coat.

2. In a large frying pan, heat oil over medium-high. Add chicken and quickly brown. Season with salt and pepper; place in a baking dish and set aside.

3. Preheat oven to 350°. Add onion to frying pan and sauté until golden; add garlic and sauté for 1 minute. Deglaze pan with wine, and simmer to reduce by half. Stir in tomatoes, garbanzos, olives, parsley and seasonings. Simmer for 5 minutes.

4. Pour sauce over chicken and bake uncovered for 30 minutes.

4 servings

Zesty Chicken

This robust chicken recipe from Sue Fellner on Guemes Island is a great company dish. Not only is it simple to prepare, but ingredients can easily be adjusted if additional friends arrive. Serve with a green salad, a full-bodied red wine and crunchy bread.

1 cup Italian salad dressing
½ teaspoon dried oregano
¼ teaspoon garlic powder
1½ pounds skinned chicken breasts or thighs, boned and cut into bite-size pieces
1 (14-ounce) can artichoke hearts, drained
1 (14-ounce) can diced stewed tomatoes, (reserve ⅓ cup liquid)
2 small zucchini, cut into ½-inch slices
1 cup pitted black olives
2 tablespoons chopped fresh parsley, garnish

1. In a large nonreactive frying pan, over medium-high heat, combine salad dressing, oregano and garlic and bring to a simmer. Add chicken and cook until done, stirring frequently.

2. Cut artichoke hearts into quarters and add to chicken. Stir in remaining ingredients and bring to a low simmer. Cook until zucchini is tender-crisp. Transfer to a heated serving dish and garnish with parsley.

4 servings

Mediterranean Chicken Fettucine

This aromatic pasta dish offers a vibrant combination of flavors. Vine-ripened tomatoes are added just before serving to create a garden fresh taste.

2 boned and skinned chicken breasts (4 breast halves)
2 tablespoons extra-virgin olive oil
½ medium red onion, diced
2-3 cloves garlic, minced
1 cup sliced mushrooms
2 tablespoons fresh minced basil or 1 teaspoon dried basil
20-ounces fettucine pasta
2 tablespoons extra-virgin olive oil
¼ cup chopped sun-dried tomatoes
¼ cup sliced calamata olives
2 tablespoons capers
½ cup dry white wine
1 cup chicken broth
4 plum tomatoes, chopped and seeded
2 tablespoons chopped fresh parsley
Salt and freshly ground pepper, to taste
½ cup grated Kasseri cheese
½ cup minced fresh Italian parsley, garnish

1. Cut chicken into bite-size pieces. In a large frying pan, heat oil over medium and sauté chicken until golden on all sides and cooked through. Remove chicken from pan and set aside.

2. Add onions, garlic, mushrooms and basil to pan and sauté until vegetables are slightly softened.

3. While vegetables are cooking, cook pasta *al dente*, according to package directions. Drain, return to pot and add oil; toss to coat. Cover to keep warm.

4. Add reserved chicken, sun-dried tomatoes, olives, capers, wine and chicken broth to onion mixture in pan and heat through.

5. Stir in plum tomatoes and parsley, and heat through, about 2 minutes. Add reserved pasta and gently toss. Salt and pepper to taste.

6. Turn pasta mixture into heated individual pasta bowls. Sprinkle with Kasseri cheese and garnish with parsley.   6 servings

Spanish Chicken and Rice

Early Spanish explorers in the San Juan Islands may have sailed with the exotic ingredients for this savory classic in the galley. A bottle of red wine, perhaps a Spanish *rioja* and a green salad will round out this eye-appealing meal.

1 (3-pound) chicken
½ teaspoon saffron threads
2 teaspoons ground cumin
½ teaspoon cayenne pepper
1 teaspoon dried oregano
1 teaspoon dried thyme
2 cloves garlic, minced
1 teaspoon salt
1 teaspoon freshly ground pepper
3 tablespoons olive oil, divided
1 medium onion, chopped
1 green bell pepper, chopped
6 bacon slices, chopped or
    4 ounces of ham, chopped
1 (15-ounce) can diced tomatoes, including juice
2 cups long-grain white rice, rinsed and drained
4 cups chicken stock
½ cup freshly grated Parmesan or Monterey Jack cheese
1 cup canned or frozen artichoke hearts, drained and sliced
1 cup frozen peas, thawed
1 tablespoon capers
⅓ cup sliced pimento green olives
¼ cup chopped fresh parsley

1. Cut chicken into serving pieces and remove skin, if desired. Rinse and pat dry; set aside. In a small bowl, combine saffron with 2 tablespoons of water and set aside to soak. In another bowl, combine next 7 ingredients (cumin through pepper) and set aside.

2. In a large heavy-bottomed casserole, over medium, heat 1 tablespoon oil. Add onion and bell pepper; sauté until vegetables are tender. Remove from pan and set aside. In same pan, sauté bacon or ham until cooked; remove from pan and set aside. Discard grease.

3. Add remaining oil to pan and increase heat to medium-high. Place chicken in pan and sprinkle with reserved herb mixture. Sauté chicken until golden on both sides, about 12 minutes. Add reserved onion, bell pepper and bacon. Add tomatoes, cover pan and cook until chicken is done, about 15-20 minutes more. Remove chicken from pan and cover to keep warm.

4. In the same pan, over medium-high, pour in rice and stir to coat. Stir in stock and bring to a boil. Reduce heat to low and add reserved saffron, including liquid. Cover and cook about 20 minutes, until rice is tender and most of the liquid is absorbed. Rice should not be dry.

5. Stir in remaining ingredients and add reserved chicken. Cover and heat until all ingredients are heated through and cheese melts. Transfer to heated individual plates. Garnish with additional parsley, if desired.

8 servings

Chicken Stuffed Chiles with Tortillas

Our friend, Dorothy Bird had a similar dish at a restaurant and after experimenting to come up with the correct flavors she shared this recipe with us. The chiles provide a wrap concentrating the complex flavors of the chicken filling. Serve with homemade tortillas, salsa and guacamole for your own fiesta.

> 1 cup uncooked brown rice
> 4 tablespoons vegetable oil, divided
> 1 cup chopped onion
> 2 cloves garlic, minced
> 1 teaspoon ground cumin
> 1 boned and skinned chicken breast, (2 halves)
> ½ cup pine nuts
> ½ cup currants, plumped in hot water
> 1 cup minced fresh cilantro
> 2 (7-ounce) cans whole green chiles
> 2 cups shredded Monterey Jack cheese
> 12 TORTILLAS (recipe follows)
> Salsa
> Guacamole

1. Prepare rice according to package directions; cover and set aside to keep warm.

2. In a medium frying pan, heat 2 tablespoons oil over medium-high and sauté onions, garlic and cumin until tender. Remove from pan and set aside.

3. Cut chicken into bite-size pieces. In same frying pan, heat remaining 2 tablespoons oil over medium-high and sauté chicken until lightly browned, about 10 minutes. Add pine nuts, stir constantly until lightly browned, about 3 minutes. Stir in reserved onion and garlic.

4. Drain currants and add to chicken mixture, stir in cilantro. Set aside.

5. Preheat oven to 350°. Spoon rice into a greased shallow baking dish.

6. Slice chiles lengthwise to create a pocket; stuff with chicken mixture. Place stuffed chiles on rice; sprinkle with cheese. Cover with foil and bake until

heated through, about 20-30 minutes. Serve with heated tortillas, salsa and guacamole.   4 servings

TORTILLAS

Homemade tortillas have a distinct flavor and aroma, they are definitely worth the effort.

> **3 cups Masa Harina***
> **1 cup unbleached white flour**
> **¼ teaspoon salt**
> **2 tablespoons corn oil**
> **2 cups warm water**

1. In a large bowl, combine masa, flour, salt and oil. Slowly add water, 1/4 cup at a time, blending with a spoon after each addition, until dough begins to ball and pull away from the side of the bowl. (Dough can be refrigerated at this time.)

2. Preheat a large frying pan to medium-high. Knead dough on a lightly floured board until smooth. Form dough into small balls, about golf-ball size.

3. Flatten balls out into 4-inch circles. On a floured board, use a rolling pin to roll dough out to 6-inch circles; add additional flour as needed. Dough will be very tender. Handle gently.

4. Cook tortillas until brown spots show on the underside; turn and cook other side. While first batch is cooking, roll out second batch. To keep tortillas warm, wrap in foil and place in warm oven.

20 tortillas

Available at Mexican and specialty markets.

Chicken and Black Bean Quesadilla

Chef Mark Abrahamson created this spicy quesadilla for the La Conner Brewing Company. It is cooked in their wood-fired oven and can be enjoyed with one of their fine brews.

CHIPOTLE PICO DE GALLO (recipe follows)
1 (12-ounce) can black beans, drained and rinsed
2 boneless chicken breast halves, baked and shredded
12 ounces pepper Jack cheese, shredded
8 (8-inch) flour tortillas
Chopped fresh cilantro, garnish
½ cup sour cream

1. Prepare Chipotle Pico De Gallo at least 45 minutes before serving time. Set aside.

2. Place beans, shredded chicken and cheese in 3 individual bowls.

3. Heat a non-stick frying pan over medium heat. Line pan with one tortilla and sprinkle with beans, chicken and cheese in desired portions. Dot with Chipotle Pico De Gallo and cover with second tortilla. Heat until bottom tortilla is crisp. Carefully turn and cook tortilla until crisp. Repeat procedure with remaining ingredients.

4. To serve, place each quesadilla on individual plates and cut into 6 wedges; sprinkle with cilantro. Serve accompanied with bowls of Chipotle Pico De Gallo and sour cream. 4 servings

CHIPOTLE PICO DE GALLO

8 Roma tomatoes, cored and cubed
½ medium red onion, minced
3 cloves garlic, minced
6 chipotle peppers, seeded and chopped
1 large bunch cilantro, chopped
3 tablespoons fresh lime juice

In a medium bowl, combine all ingredients. Toss well, cover and allow to sit for 45 minutes before serving. 2 cups

Bathing Rama

The name of this traditional Thai dish suggests that it was created in honor of a king (Rama). "Bathing" describes the way the chicken is presented, floating over the greens in a rich sauce. We prefer to stir-fry the chicken rather than the traditional method of cooking it in the sauce. The ingredients are available at Asian markets and most grocery stores.

Peanut Sauce
- 1 (14-ounce) can light coconut milk
- ½ cup peanut butter
- ½ cup chicken stock
- 2 tablespoons minced fresh lemongrass
- 3 cloves garlic, minced
- 1 teaspoon salt
- 1 tablespoon palm or brown sugar
- 2 tablespoons Thai fish sauce or soy sauce
- ¼ cup freshly squeezed lime juice
- 2 dried red chilies, seeded and finely chopped or
- 2 teaspoons red pepper flakes
- 2 boned and skinned chicken breasts (4 breast halves)
- 1 tablespoon peanut oil
- 2 bunches fresh spinach, cleaned and stems removed
- 6 cups cooked Jasmine rice

1. Prepare Peanut Sauce: In a saucepan, over medium heat, bring coconut milk to a boil. Simmer about 5 minutes, stirring constantly.

2. Add peanut butter, stock, lemongrass, garlic, salt and sugar; stir until smooth and thick, about 5 minutes. Stir in fish sauce, lime juice, red chilies; reduce heat to low. Adjust seasonings to desired degree of "hot."

3. Cut chicken into thin strips. In a wok, over medium-high, heat oil and stir-fry chicken in two batches. Cook chicken until done, about 7 minutes.

4. Stir chicken into Peanut Sauce. Add spinach to wok, cover and steam in meat juices, about 3 minutes. Spinach should be slightly wilted; do not overcook.

5. Place spinach on heated serving dish, pour Peanut Sauce with chicken over spinach. Serve with steamed rice.   4-6 servings

Chicken, Walnuts
And Gorgonzola with Pasta

Toasted walnuts add a crunchy contrast to the rich creamy Gorgonzola sauce.

1 ¼ cups walnut halves, divided
2 boned and skinned chicken breasts (4 breast halves)
5 tablespoons vegetable oil, divided
1 (16-ounce) package fettucine pasta
3 tablespoons butter
4 ounces Gorgonzola cheese (1 cup crumbled)
1 cup milk
1 cup light or heavy cream
Salt and freshly ground pepper, to taste

1. Preheat oven to 325°. Place walnut halves in shallow baking dish and toast until lightly browned, about 7 minutes. Remove from oven and allow to cool. With a sharp knife, coarsely chop and set aside.

2. Cut chicken into bite-size pieces. In a large frying pan, over medium high, heat 3 tablespoons oil and sauté chicken until done. Remove from pan and set aside.

3. In a large pot, cook pasta al dente, according to package directions. Drain, return to pot and add remaining 2 tablespoons oil; toss to coat. Cover to keep warm.

4. While pasta is cooking, in a small saucepan over low heat, combine butter, Gorgonzola, milk and cream. Stir until cheese and butter melt and sauce has a creamy consistency, about 6 minutes.

5. Increase heat to medium, stir and cook until sauce is reduced by one-fourth; do not boil. Add chicken and 1 cup of the walnuts to sauce; heat through.

6. Pour sauce over reserved pasta and gently toss. Salt and pepper to taste. Turn pasta mixture into heated individual pasta bowls. Sprinkle with remaining 1/4 cup walnuts.   4 servings

Artichoke Primavera

Gere-a-Deli in Anacortes is known for its Friday night pastas. This is one of proprietor Laurie Gere's most popular sauces. You will surely delight in the savory combination of flavors particularly if you are able to enjoy it with a glass of "cheap red wine," Gere-a-Deli style.

¼ cup olive oil
2 cups diced onions
2 tablespoons minced garlic
½ teaspoon oregano
¼ teaspoon dried red pepper flakes
½ teaspoon salt
1 tablespoon freshly ground black pepper
¾ cup herbed Italian salad dressing
1 (28-ounce) can chopped plum tomatoes, including juice
1½ pounds angel hair or penne pasta
1 (12-ounce) can water-packed artichoke hearts, drained
2 tablespoons chopped fresh basil
    or 1 teaspoon dried basil
¼ cup chopped fresh cilantro
¼ cup chopped fresh Italian parsley
1 cup freshly grated Parmesan cheese
Parmesan cheese, garnish

1. In a large frying pan, warm oil over medium heat and sauté onion and garlic until softened. Add herbs, seasonings, Italian dressing and tomatoes with juice; simmer for 15 minutes.

2. While tomato sauce is cooking, in a large pot, cook pasta al dente, according to package directions. Drain, return to pot and add 2 tablespoons olive oil; toss to coat. Cover to keep warm.

3. Stir in artichoke hearts, basil, cilantro and parsley; simmer for 5 minutes to blend flavors and heat through. Add to pasta and toss to coat.

4. Just before serving, stir in Parmesan. Turn pasta mixture onto heated individual plates and serve with additional Parmesan.　　6 servings

Garden Cafe Panang

Chef Libi Zderic created this spicy Thai vegetable curry for the Garden Cafe in Eastsound on Orcas Island. It is an aromatic and flavorful topping for Chinese noodles, Jasmine or brown rice.

½ cup canola oil, divided
2 onions, chopped
2-4 cloves garlic, minced
2 red bell peppers, julienned
½ pound fresh mushrooms, sliced
2 red potatoes, cubed
2 cups uncooked rice
2 tablespoons Thai red curry paste (*available at local markets or specialty stores*)
2 (14-ounce) cans coconut milk
1½ teaspoons sucanat or brown sugar
2 tablespoons arrowroot powder
Salt and freshly ground pepper, to taste
½ cup chopped peanuts, garnish
¼ cup chopped fresh cilantro, garnish
1 cup Mung bean sprouts, garnish

1. In a large frying pan, heat 1/4 cup oil over medium-high and sauté onions, garlic, red peppers and mushrooms until tender. Remove from heat.

2. While vegetables are cooking, in a small saucepan, boil potatoes until tender but still firm. Drain and set aside.

3. Cook rice according to package directions; keep warm.

4. In a large saucepan, over medium heat, combine remaining 1/4 cup oil and red curry paste. Whisk constantly for 2 to 3 minutes; do not burn. Add coconut milk and bring mixture to a slow boil.

5. Add all vegetables and sweetener to coconut milk mixture and simmer to meld flavors, about 4 minutes.

6. In a small bowl, dissolve arrowroot in 2 tablespoons of water. Add to vegetable sauce; continue stirring until sauce thickens.

7. Spoon rice into individual shallow soup bowls and top with vegetable curry sauce. Garnish with peanuts, cilantro and sprouts.   4 servings

Skagit Garden Fettucine

Fresh vegetables are the key to this flavorful dish, created by Chef Rich Aguilar, for the Anacortes Brewhouse. Enjoy one of their excellent micro-brews that are made on the premises. As the seasons change, so does their menu as well as their brew offerings. It is a great place to get together with friends.

1 red bell pepper, julienned
1 green bell pepper, julienned
2 carrots, peeled and julienned
1 zucchini, julienned
½ head cauliflower, cut into florets
½ head broccoli, cut into florets
16 snow peas or snap peas (optional)
½ medium red onion, slivered
4 cloves garlic, minced
1 (12-ounce) package fettucine pasta
4 tablespoons extra-virgin olive oil, divided
6 leaves fresh basil, minced,
       or 2 teaspoons dried basil
1 teaspoon dried oregano
½ cup dry white wine
Salt and freshly ground pepper, to taste
2 plum tomatoes, seeded and diced, garnish
½ cup freshly grated Parmesan cheese, garnish

1. Cut vegetables as described and combine in a large bowl; set aside.

2. In a large pot, cook pasta al dente according to package directions; drain and return to pot. Add 2 tablespoons oil and toss to coat. Cover to keep warm.

3. While pasta is cooking, in a large frying pan, heat remaining 2 tablespoons oil over medium-high. Sauté all vegetables and herbs until vegetables are tender-crisp, about 10 to 15 minutes. Add wine and heat through.

4. Add vegetable mixture to cooked fettucine; toss gently. Salt and pepper to taste. Heat through to blend flavors.

5. Turn pasta mixture onto heated individual plates. Garnish with tomatoes and Parmesan cheese. Serve immediately.   4-6 servings

Hot Chile and Corn Pot Pie

At San Juan Island's Duck Soup Inn, Chef Gretchen Allison draws on the traditionally vegetarian cuisine of Mexico to create this delectable pie, varying the vegetables to suit the season. Long cooking vegetables need to be grilled, sautéed or parboiled before assembling the pies.

    1 sweet potato
    1 parsnip
    1 eggplant, sliced ½-inch thick
    1 teaspoon salt
    5 tablespoons olive oil, divided
    4 hot chiles, seeded and sliced
    2 cloves garlic, minced
    2 onions, sliced
    Salt and freshly ground pepper, to taste
    4 cobs fresh corn, raw
    3 zucchini, grated
    3 tomatoes, sliced
    3 cups grated mozzarella cheese
    ½ cup chopped fresh basil leaves
    CORNBREAD CRUST (recipe follows)
    ¼ cup cornmeal
    Sour cream, garnish

1. In a medium saucepan, boil potato and parsnip until tender. Cool, peel and slice into 1/4-inch thick slices; set aside.

2. Sprinkle eggplant slices with salt and place in a colander to drain bitter juices, about 20 minutes. Pat dry with paper towel. Drizzle slices with 2 tablespoons oil. In a large frying pan, sauté eggplant until lightly browned on both sides. Remove from pan and set aside.

3. Preheat oven to 350°. Add remaining 3 tablespoons oil to frying pan and sauté chiles, garlic and onions until lightly browned. Salt and pepper to taste. With a sharp knife, remove corn kernels from cobs and set aside.

4. In a large bowl, combine all vegetables: Sweet potato, parsnip, eggplant, chiles, garlic, onions, corn, zucchini and tomatoes.

5. Assemble pies: In individual greased casserole dishes, alternate layers of

vegetable mixture with grated cheese and fresh basil leaves.

6. Cover each pie with foil and bake until cooked through, about 1 hour.

7. While pies are cooking, prepare Cornbread Crust, according to directions.

8. Remove pies from oven. Increase oven temperature to 500°.

9. Remove foil and top each pie with 1/4-inch thick layer of corn batter. Sprinkle each pie with a little cornmeal. Return pies to oven and bake 10 to 15 minutes, until lightly browned. Serve with sour cream.

8-10 servings

CORNBREAD CRUST

¾ cup water
⅓ cup coarse cornmeal
½ cup pureed fresh corn
½ tablespoon orange zest
¼ cup vegetable oil
½ teaspoon salt
⅓ cup milk
¼ teaspoon baking powder
1 cup all-purpose flour

In a medium saucepan, over low heat, combine water and cornmeal; stir and simmer for 2 minutes. Remove from heat and stir in remaining ingredients.

Mediterranean Marinara Sauce

This fresh-flavored, versatile sauce can be served over polenta, eggplant, chicken, fish or pasta.

3 tablespoons extra-virgin olive oil
3 cloves garlic, minced
8 mushrooms, quartered
1½ teaspoons dried oregano
1½ teaspoons dried basil
½ teaspoon red pepper flakes
1 cup dry white wine
1 (28-ounce) can diced tomatoes in puree
1 (14½-ounce) can diced tomatoes in puree
½ cup sliced calamata olives
1 (6-ounce) jar marinated artichoke hearts, drained and sliced
½ teaspoon sugar
Salt and freshly ground pepper, to taste

1. In a large heavy-bottomed pot, heat oil over medium. Lightly sauté garlic, mushrooms and seasonings, about 5 minutes.

2. Pour in wine and simmer for about 10 minutes. Add tomatoes, olives, artichoke hearts and sugar. With lid ajar, continue to simmer 20 more minutes, stirring occasionally.

3. Add salt and pepper to taste. Sauce can be used immediately or refrigerate for several days.

6 cups

Chile Relleno Pie

Cafe Olga and the Orcas Island Artworks are located in a picturesque strawberry-packing barn built in the 1930s. It is a favorite gathering place for local folks and tourists who delight in both the delectable food and the quality island art.

3 cups water
¼ cup red wine
½ teaspoon salt
2 teaspoons chili powder
1 cup uncooked coarse cornmeal
2 (7-ounce) cans whole green roasted chilies
1 to 1½ cups shredded Cheddar cheese
4 eggs, beaten
1 cup light cream
½ teaspoon red pepper flakes
1 teaspoon salt
¼ teaspoon freshly ground pepper

1. In a saucepan, over high heat, bring water, wine, salt and chili powder to a boil. Reduce heat to simmer and slowly add cornmeal, stirring constantly. Continue to cook over medium-low heat, stirring frequently. Cook until creamy, about 5 minutes.

2. Preheat oven to 375°. Spread polenta into the bottom of a 7 x 11-inch baking dish and set aside.

3. Stuff chilies with a heaping tablespoon of cheese. Place the stuffed chilies on top of polenta.

4. In a medium bowl, combine remaining ingredients. Pour mixture over stuffed chilies. Bake about 35 minutes, until set and golden brown.

4 servings

Hungarian Winter Pies

We were delighted that Chef Michael Stark agreed to share this old family recipe with us. Highlighting root vegetables, these pies are a perfect winter meal. A creamy sauce spiked with saurkraut and horseradish sets off the sweetness of the lamb.

¼ cup vegetable oil
3 pounds boned leg of lamb, cubed
1 medium onion, sliced
1 cup sour cream
1½ cups sauerkraut
2 teaspoons Hungarian paprika
¼ cup white wine vinegar
3 medium carrots, peeled and diced
2 medium parsnips, peeled and diced
1 medium rutabaga, peeled and diced
1 medium turnip, peeled and diced
Salt and freshly ground pepper, to taste
2 -3 teaspoons prepared horseradish
1½ boxes frozen puff pastry (3 sheets)*
1 egg, beaten with 1 teaspoon water

1. In a large heavy pan, heat oil over medium-high; brown lamb in two batches. Return all meat to pan and add onion, reduce heat, and add 1/2 cup water. Cover and cook 20 minutes. Add more water as needed, to prevent sticking.

2. Stir sour cream, sauerkraut and paprika into simmering lamb. Cover and continue cooking until lamb is tender, about 15 minutes.

3. While lamb is cooking, in medium pot, boil vegetables in salted water until tender-crisp. In a colander, drain vegetables and rinse with cold water to prevent further cooking.

4. Add vegetables to the lamb mixture. Season with salt and pepper. Stir in horseradish, for an added zip. If the mixture is too soupy, thicken by cooking for 5 minutes more, uncovered.

5. Preheat oven to 350°. Spoon lamb mixture into 8 individual rarebit boats (individual casseroles).

6. Roll out puff pastry about 1/4-inch thick. Cut pastry to just overlap edges of dishes. Lay over lamb mixture and seal edges.

7. Brush beaten egg wash over each pie. Bake until browned, about 15 minutes.

8 servings

Available in the frozen food section of most grocery stores.

San Juan Island Jazz Festival Crepes

Every July, San Juan Island hosts a Jazz Festival. For years, Pat DeStaffany, owner of the popular kitchen shop, Gourmets' Galley, prepared 300 of these crepes for the musicians. While they are no longer served, they are still well-remembered.

Crepe Batter
   1½ cups milk
   3 eggs
   3 tablespoons butter, melted
   1½ cups all-purpose flour
   ¼ teaspoon salt
3 tablespoons butter, for frying

Crepe Filling
   3 tablespoons vegetable oil
   1 medium onion, chopped
   1 pound mushrooms, sliced
   3 to 4 zucchini or crookneck squash, sliced
   1 green or red bell pepper, chopped
   ½ cup vermouth

Béarnaise Sauce
   4 egg yolks
   2 tablespoons fresh lemon juice
   2 tablespoons capers
   2 teaspoons dried tarragon
   2 teaspoons tarragon vinegar
   2 tablespoons dried parsley flakes
   1½ cups unsalted butter, melted

1. Prepare crepe batter several hours in advance and refrigerate. In a blender combine milk, eggs and butter; mix on low speed. With the motor running, add flour and salt; blend until smooth.

2. In a 6-to 8-inch crepe pan, melt 1 teaspoon butter over medium heat. Coat pan surface with butter. Pour 2 tablespoons batter into pan and tilt to cover pan bottom with a thin layer. Cook crepe until edges are lightly browned and surface appears dry, about 45 seconds. Turn and cook other

side about 15 seconds. Remove from pan and place on a plate; cover with foil to keep warm. Repeat procedure until all the batter is used. (Crepes can be made up to 2 days ahead and refrigerated, or made ahead and frozen.)

3. Prepare filling: In a large frying pan, over medium, heat oil and sauté vegetables until tender, about 8 to 10 minutes. Deglaze pan with vermouth and set aside.

4. Prepare Béarnaise Sauce: Using a blender, at low speed, mix first 6 ingredients thoroughly. Slowly add melted butter and blend until thick. Set aside.

5. Preheat oven to 350°. Place about 1/2 cup filling on each crepe. Roll crepe and place in a buttered shallow baking dish with seam down. Continue with remaining crepes and filling. Spoon sauce over crepes and warm in oven.   12-14 crepes

Pesto Pizza with Fire-Roasted Peppers

Beautifully appointed, La Conner Brewing Company features unique house-brewed ales and hand-tossed pizzas using local produce and seafood. Chef Mark Abrahamson finishes this eye-appealing pizza in an applewood-fired oven.

Pizza Dough, 4 (8-to 10-inch) crusts
- 2¼ teaspoons dry yeast
- 1 cup warm water, divided
- 2 teaspoons salt
- 3 tablespoons olive oil
- 2 tablespoons honey
- 3 cups unbleached white flour

PESTO SAUCE (recipe follows)

Topping
- 2 tablespoons olive oil
- 1 large clove garlic
- 8 sun-dried tomatoes, julienned
- 6 ounces goat cheese, crumbled
- 4 artichoke hearts, quartered
- 2 roasted red peppers, julienned
- 2 roasted yellow peppers, julienned

1. In a small bowl, dissolve yeast in 1/4 cup warm water to proof for about 10 minutes.

2. In a large mixing bowl, combine remaining 3/4 cup water, salt, oil and honey. Add flour, one cup at a time, mix for 2 minutes and add yeast liquid. Continue mixing for about 8 minutes or until dough begins to ball and pull away from side of bowl. Dough should be smooth and elastic; add additional flour as necessary to prevent sticking.

3. Remove dough from bowl and place on a floured surface. Divide into four equal portions and roll into balls. Cover with a damp towel and let rise at room temperature for 1 hour. (Dough is best if made a day ahead. Cover with plastic and refrigerate overnight before rising.)

4. While dough is rising, prepare Pesto Sauce, if not made ahead. Prepare topping ingredients and set aside.

5. Place oven rack in the lowest position and preheat oven to 500°.

6. For a thin, crispy crust, use a rolling pin to roll out each dough ball to an 8-to 10-inch circle. For a more rustic crust, use your fingers and flatten the dough from the center outwards, until it is bowl-shaped with a rim around the edge. Using your thumb and forefinger stretch the dough to form an 8-to 10-inch circle. (Handle the rim as little as possible to allow for maximum rising.) If you are adventurous, try throwing the dough until round, as the professionals do.

7. Place 2 of the crusts on a perforated baking sheet. (Bake the remaining pizzas after the first have cooked.) Rub each crust with oil and garlic. Place a heaping tablespoon of Pesto Sauce in the center of each crust and distribute in a circle with the back of spoon.

8. Cover each pizza evenly with one-quarter of remaining topping ingredients: tomatoes, cheese, artichokes and peppers. Bake for 6 minutes or until crust edges and bottoms are golden brown.   4 pizzas

PESTO SAUCE
This sauce can be made several days ahead.

> 2 cups fresh chopped basil
> 3 cloves garlic
> 1 teaspoon anchovy paste
> 3 sprigs fresh parsley
> 2 tablespoons pine nuts
> ¼ cup freshly grated Parmesan cheese
> ¼ teaspoon salt
> ¼ teaspoon freshly ground pepper
> 1 tablespoon freshly squeezed lemon juice
> 2 tablespoons olive oil

In a food processor, combine all ingredients and mix thoroughly. Remove and place in a jar. Top with a thin layer of oil to prevent discoloring; cover and refrigerate.

Pueblo Polenta

Proprieters and Chefs Chuck Silva and Karen Campbell Silva of Chimayo, a Mexican restaurant in Eastsound, on Orcas Island, serve this delicious polenta. The dining room is painted to resemble the inside of an Anazasi cliff dwelling, complete with sandstone walls and petroglyphs.

> 5 cups water
> 1 teaspoon salt
> 3 cups coarse cornmeal, soaked in 2 cups water
> 1 cup grated Cheddar cheese
> 1 cup grated Monterey Jack cheese
> 2 teaspoons ground cumin seed
> 2 teaspoons Mexican oregano
> 1 teaspoon paprika
> 1 teaspoon pepper
> 2 cups frozen corn, divided
> 2 fresh tomatoes, sliced and halved
> 1 (8-ounce) can diced green chiles
> 1 cup grated Jack and Cheddar cheese, combined
> 2 (14-ounce) cans Chipotle enchilada sauce
> 1 cup chopped fresh cilantro, garnish

1. Allow cornmeal to soak in 2 cups water for a few minutes. In a saucepan, over high heat, bring 5 cups water and salt to a boil. Reduce heat to a simmer and slowly add cornmeal, stirring constantly. Continue to cook over low heat, stirring frequently. Cook until mixture is thick and creamy, about 10 minutes. Remove from heat and stir in cheeses, seasonings and 1 1/2 cups corn. Preheat oven to 375°.

2. Grease a 9 x 13-inch pan and spoon in polenta. With a spatula, spread into a smooth layer. Top polenta with sliced tomatoes, chiles, remaining corn and cheese. Dust with additional oregano and cumin.

3. Bake polenta for 45 minutes. Remove from oven and allow to set up for 15 minutes before cutting.

4. In a medium pan, over medium, heat enchilada sauce and keep warm. Serve polenta squares on a pool of warm sauce and sprinkle with cilantro.

8-10 servings

Pork Tenderloin with Apple Brandy

Fidalgo Island's La Petite Restaurant has received an excellent ranking in the book, Northwest Best Places since 1983. This intimate restaurant offers eclectic cuisine using only the freshest of ingredients. Chef Derek Beck created this recipe using Washington's Gala apples, in season from mid-September to November and known for their sweetness.

    2 pounds pork tenderloin
    Salt and freshly ground pepper
    2 tablespoons olive oil
    4 tablespoons butter, divided
    1 tablespoon chopped shallots
    1 Gala apple, skinned, cored and quartered
    3 ounces Laird's Applejack Brandy
    ⅔ cup chicken stock
    1 teaspoon fresh lemon juice
    ⅔ cup heavy cream
    1 teaspoon chopped parsley
    Salt and freshly ground pepper, to taste

1. Preheat oven to 350°. Salt and pepper tenderloin and set aside. In a large frying pan, over medium-high, heat oil and add 2 tablespoons butter. When butter has browned, but not burned, add whole pork tenderloin, sear on all sides. Set pork in roasting pan and finish cooking in oven until done, about 20 minutes.

2. While pork is cooking, add remaining 2 tablespoons butter to frying pan. Over high heat, add shallots and apples, turning constantly until shallots begin to caramelize. Reduce heat to low and remove apples and shallots; cover to keep warm.

3. Add brandy to frying pan. Keep area clear and use caution; ignite brandy. When flames subside, add chicken stock and lemon juice. Continue cooking to reduce liquid by half. Stir in cream and parsley; reduce until sauce coats the back of a spoon. Add salt and pepper to taste. Just before serving, return apples and shallots to sauce; heat through. Slice pork and place on individual heated plates. Cover with apple brandy sauce. Serve immediately.

4 servings

Smoked Pork Chops With Lingonberry Sauce

This combination, devised by Executive Chef Kevin Sykes, of Rosario Resort on Orca Island, is another example of his imaginative cuisine. His dedication to detail and the impeccable care he takes in recipe development and plate presentation is evident in the appeal of his menu offerings.

ROSEMARY POTATO PANCAKES (recipe follows)
1 tablespoon butter
4 smoked pork chops
1 tablespoon chopped shallots
½ cup red wine
1 (8-ounce) can chicken stock
1 tablespoon Dijon mustard
¼ cup lingonberry preserves
4 rosemary sprigs, garnish

1. Complete steps 1 and 2 of Rosemary Potato Pancakes.

2. Preheat oven to 325°. In a large frying pan, over medium-high heat, melt butter. Sear pork chops about 2 to 3 minutes on each side. Transfer chops to a platter and place in oven; heat through.

3. While pork chops are in the oven, prepare sauce. In same frying pan, add shallots and sauté. Deglaze pan with red wine. Blend in stock, mustard and preserves; heat through. Turn heat to low and cover to keep warm. Remove chops from oven, cover and allow to rest.

4. Finish Rosemary Potato Pancakes by completing steps 3 and 4).

5. To serve, place potato pancake on heated individual plate and top with pork chop. Spoon sauce over chop and garnish with a rosemary sprig. Repeat procedure for remaining servings. Serve immediately.

4 servings

ROSEMARY POTATO PANCAKES

1½ pounds russet potatoes, grated
1 cup grated onion
1 tablespoon chopped fresh rosemary
½ teaspoon salt
⅛ teaspoon freshly ground pepper
¼ cup vegetable oil

1. Place potatoes in a colander for 15 to 20 minutes. Potatoes will release liquid and turn red.

2. In a medium bowl, combine onion, rosemary, salt and pepper; set aside.

3. Rinse potatoes with cold running water; red starch will wash out. Squeeze out as much liquid as possible. Stir potatoes into onion mixture.

4. In a large frying pan, over medium-high, heat oil. Using a large slotted spoon, drop 4 spoonfuls of potato mixture into hot oil. Fry until golden brown and turn to brown other side. Remove from pan and place on paper towel to remove excess oil. Repeat with remaining potato pancake mixture.   4-8 pancakes

Rigatoni with White Beans and Sausage

This attractive pasta dish provides a delectable combination of creamy beans and spicy sausage laced with tomatoes.

1 cup dry white Cannellini or Great Northern beans
12 ounces small rigatoni or penne pasta
3 tablespoon extra-virgin olive oil, divided
2-3 cloves garlic, minced
1 pound Italian link sausage, sliced into bite-size pieces
1 (28-ounce) can diced plum tomatoes, drained and reserving liquid
15 fresh sage leaves, chopped
Salt and pepper, to taste
Sage leaves, garnish

1. In a colander, rinse beans. Place beans in a medium saucepan, add cold water to cover. Let soak overnight.

2. Drain beans and return to pan with enough fresh water to measure 2 inches above beans. Bring to a boil, reduce heat to low and simmer, covered, 30 minutes. With lid ajar, continue simmering until the skins begin to crack and the beans are tender, about 30 minutes more. (Taste the beans periodically. When done, they should feel creamy in your mouth.) Drain and rinse in cold water; set aside.

3. In a large pot, cook pasta al dente, according to package directions. Drain, return to pot and add 2 tablespoons oil; toss to coat. Cover to keep warm.

4. In a large frying pan, over medium, heat 1 tablespoon oil and sauté garlic about 1 minute. Add sausage and brown. Stir in tomatoes; add sage and reserved beans. With lid ajar, simmer for 15 minutes.

5. Add reserved pasta to sausage mixture, gently toss to coat. If mixture seems dry, add reserved tomato liquid, as needed; heat through, about 2 minutes. Salt and pepper, to taste. Serve in individual heated pasta bowls, and garnish with fresh sage.   6 servings

Calzone

Calzone may have started out as folded-over pizza, but they have come into their own. We offer a choice of three fillings. It's fun to experiment with different fillings, but take care that they are not too moist. Moisture creates steam, causing the crust to be soggy.

    1½ teaspoons dry yeast
    1 cup warm water (about 110°)
    1 tablespoon honey
    1½ teaspoons salt
    2¾ to 3 cups unbleached white flour
    2 tablespoons melted butter
    SPINACH FILLING (recipe follows)
    SAUSAGE FILLING (recipe follows)
    PROSCIUTTO FILLING (recipe follows)

1. In a large mixing bowl, sprinkle yeast over warm water. Add honey and stir gently to mix. Let stand for 5 minutes to proof.

2. Stir in salt and gradually mix in flour to make a soft dough. Turn out onto a well-floured board and knead until smooth and non-sticky. Add additional flour as needed.

3. Place dough in a greased bowl; turn to grease top. Cover and set in a warm place to rise until doubled (about 1 hour).

4. Prepare Filling while dough rises; set aside.

5. Preheat oven to 450°. After dough has risen, punch it down and divide into six equal portions. Roll into balls. With a rolling pin, roll out each ball into a circle, 1/4-inch thick. Place 1/2 to 3/4 cup of the filling onto one side of the circle, leaving a 1/2-inch rim. Do not overfill the calzone or it may split when baking.

6. Dip fingertips in a bowl of water and moisten the rim. Fold the other side of the dough over filling. Crimp the edge with a fork. Prick the top of the calzone with the fork. Bake on a greased baking sheet for 15-20 minutes, or until crisp and lightly-browned. Remove from oven and brush each pastry with butter.   6 calzones

SPINACH FILLING

½ pound fresh spinach, cleaned and stems removed
1 tablespoon butter
¼ cup minced onion
1 clove garlic, minced
1 (8-ounce) container ricotta cheese
1½ cups grated mozzarella cheese
¼ cup freshly grated Parmesan cheese
Dash of nutmeg
Salt and freshly ground pepper, to taste

1. In a medium saucepan, over medium-high heat, steam spinach in 1 inch of water. Drain spinach and place in large bowl; set aside.

2. In a small frying pan, over medium, melt butter and sauté onion and garlic until soft. Add onion mixture and remaining ingredients to spinach, and stir to combine. Salt and pepper to taste.

SAUSAGE FILLING

3 Italian sausages, sliced
1 small onion, chopped
1 clove garlic, minced
¼ pound mushrooms, sliced
½ red bell pepper, diced
½ cup sliced black olives
¾ cup sliced artichoke hearts
1 (8-ounce) can tomato sauce
1 teaspoon dried basil
½ teaspoon dried oregano
½ teaspoon sugar
1½ cups grated mozzarella cheese
½ cup freshly grated Parmesan cheese
Salt and freshly ground pepper, to taste

1. In a medium frying pan, cook sausage until browned and cooked through. Remove sausage from pan and discard all but 1 tablespoon of fat. Add onion, garlic, mushrooms and peppers to frying pan and sauté until vegetables are tender.

2. Stir in olives, artichokes, tomato sauce and seasonings to pan and simmer about 5 minutes. Remove from heat and let cool.

3. Add mozzarella, Parmesan and salt and pepper to taste.

PROSCIUTTO FILLING

1½ cups grated mozzarella cheese
¾ cup ricotta cheese
1 cup freshly grated Parmesan cheese
2 ounces prosciutto, julienned
¼ cup sliced calamata olives
1 medium ripe tomato, chopped and seeded
¼ cup chopped fresh parsley
1 teaspoon dried basil
Salt and freshly ground pepper, to taste

In a medium bowl, combine all ingredients. Salt and pepper to taste.

Herb-Crusted Rack of Lamb
With Saffron Rice

Overlooking Friday Harbor, Maloula Restaurant offers one of the best views of the busy marina from their outdoor deck. This is one of the most popular entrees from the authentic bill of fare offered by the Nassarallah family in their warm and friendly restaurant.

2 racks of lamb, cut in half and trimmed of fat
2 tablespoons olive oil
2 cloves garlic, minced
1 teaspoon salt
1 teaspoon allspice
Herb Crust
    2 cups chopped fresh parsley
    Zest of ½ lemon
    4 cloves garlic, minced
    2 tablespoons seasoned breadcrumbs
    2 tablespoons chopped fresh sage
    ⅓ cup olive oil
12 button mushrooms, halved
2 medium zucchini, cut into ½-inch slices
1 red bell pepper, cut into 1-inch cubes
1 tablespoon olive oil
1½ teaspoons dried oregano
Salt and freshly ground pepper
SAFFRON RICE (recipe follows)

1. Preheat oven to 350°. Rinse and dry lamb. Rub meat with olive oil and sprinkle with garlic, salt and allspice. Arrange the lamb racks on a baking sheet and cook for 10 minutes.

2. While lamb is baking, prepare Herb Crust. In a small bowl, combine parsley, lemon zest, garlic, breadcrumbs, sage and oil and mix to the consistency of thick paste. Add more oil, if necessary.

3. Remove lamb from oven and spread the Herb Crust to cover each rack. Arrange vegetables around lamb and sprinkle with olive oil, oregano, salt and pepper.

4. Return lamb to oven and cook 25 to 30 minutes more for medium; or continue to cook longer if you prefer lamb well done. Remove from oven and cover to keep warm. While lamb is cooking, prepare Saffron Rice.

5. Transfer lamb, vegetables and rice to heated individual plates and serve.

4 servings

SAFFRON RICE

1 tablespoon olive oil
1 carrot, finely diced
2 cups long-grain rice
½ teaspoon saffron threads
4 cups water
1½ teaspoons salt

1. In a large saucepan, over medium, heat oil and sauté carrots about 2 minutes. Add rice and saffron; sauté an additional minute.

2. Add water and salt, increase heat to high and bring water to a boil. Reduce heat to low, cover and cook rice according to package directions; fluff with a fork.   4 servings

Island Lamb Shanks

Sharron Prosser serves these delectable lamb shanks with her Bistro Potatoes. Long, slow cooking brings out the flavor in these lamb shanks embellished with a rich tomato wine sauce flavored with oregano and cinnamon.

>   4 lamb shanks, fat well-trimmed
>   1 teaspoon dry mustard
>   Salt and freshly ground pepper
>   1 large onion, thinly sliced
>   1 (8-ounce) can tomato sauce
>   1 clove garlic, minced
>   ½ cup dry white wine
>   ½ teaspoon salt
>   ½ teaspoon dried oregano
>   ¼ teaspoon ground cinnamon
>   ¼ teaspoon sugar
>   1½ teaspoons chopped lemon zest, garnish
>   2 tablespoons chopped Italian parsley, garnish

1. Preheat oven to 350°. Place lamb shanks in a roasting pan or large casserole with lid. Sprinkle lamb with mustard, salt and pepper. Spread onion slices over the top.

2. In medium bowl, combine next 7 ingredients and pour over lamb. Cover and bake 2 1/2 hours, or until very tender. Remove from oven.

3. While lamb is cooking, prepare Bistro Potatoes on page 185, if desired.

4. Transfer lamb shanks to individual, warmed plates. Skim fat from the pan juices. Place shanks on mashed potatoes or a bed of wide egg noodles and top with sauce. Garnish with lemon zest and parsley.

4 servings

Lopez Lamb Curry

Lopez Island offers serene, pastoral views of sheep grazing on gently sloping fields. Chicken or prawns can be substituted for lamb in this aromatic, spicy dish. Serve on scented Jasmine rice for additional flavor.

    2 tablespoons extra-virgin olive oil
    ½ cup chopped onion
    2 cloves garlic, minced
    1 tablespoon minced fresh ginger
    1 tablespoon ground coriander
    1 teaspoon ground cumin
    ½ teaspoon ground cardamom
    ½ teaspoon ground turmeric
    ¼ teaspoon cayenne pepper
    1½ pounds lamb shoulder, cut into 1-inch pieces
    1½ cups chicken stock
    ½ cup tomato puree
    1 cinnamon stick
    1 teaspoon salt
    ¼ teaspoon freshly ground pepper
    ½ cup yogurt
    6 cups cooked Jasmine rice
    Toasted coconut, golden raisins, chutney, peanuts (condiments)

1. In a large frying pan, heat oil over medium. Sauté onion, garlic and spices until onions are tender, about 5 minutes.

2. Add lamb and sauté until lightly browned on all sides, about 10-15 minutes.

3. Add remaining ingredients, except yogurt. Cover pan with lid ajar and simmer curry for 30 to 40 minutes. While curry is cooking, prepare rice.

4. Discard cinnamon stick. Just before serving, remove pan from heat and stir in yogurt.

5. Serve curry over rice and offer bowls of condiments at the table.

4 servings

Grilled Steak
With Peppercorn or Béarnaise Sauce

There is nothing better than the smoky flavor of a steak cooked over an outdoor grill. Choose one of these sauces as a tasty complement. Always handle beef with tongs, to prevent piercing the meat, allowing juices to escape. The beef will continue to cook after it is taken off the grill so it is best to remove the meat a few minutes before the cooking time is completed.

4 (1-inch thick) beef steaks, at room temperature
PEPPERCORN SAUCE (recipe follows)
BÉARNAISE SAUCE (recipe follows)

1. Prepare Peppercorn or Béarnaise Sauce following directions.

2. Preheat grill on high until the metal surface is very hot, so meat is immediately seared and marked. Lightly oil grill. Place steak on grill and close lid. Reduce heat to medium and grill steak.

3. Turn steak only once, using tongs. Cooking time will vary according to the thickness of the steak. (For a 1-inch thick steak, total cooking time should be about 10 minutes for rare.) Remember, the steak will continue to cook after it is removed from grill. It is best to remove meat from heat source before you consider it done.

4. Transfer steaks to heated plates, and allow to rest for about 5 minutes before serving to allow juices to settle in the meat. Accompany the steaks with the sauce of your choice, or season with salt and pepper and serve.

4 servings

PEPPERCORN SAUCE

  1 tablespoon butter
  2 garlic cloves, minced
  1½ tablespoons cracked peppercorn-blend pepper*
  ¼ cup tarragon vinegar, or white dry wine
  ¼ cup Dijon mustard
  2 cups heavy cream

1. In a small saucepan, over medium, heat butter and sauté garlic about 1 minute. Add peppercorns and vinegar, bring to a boil, reduce heat and simmer until liquid is reduced to a few spoonful.

2. Add mustard and cream and cook, stirring constantly, until sauce is reduced by half. Remove from heat and cover to keep warm while broiling steak. (Sauce can be made two days in advance and refrigerated. Reheat, over medium, before using.)   1 1/4 cups

Available in the spice section of most grocery stores.

BÉARNAISE SAUCE

  ¼ cup white wine vinegar
  ¼ cup dry white wine
  1 tablespoon minced shallots
  1 teaspoon dried tarragon or
      1 tablespoon chopped fresh tarragon
  3 egg yolks, beaten
  ¾ cup butter, melted
  Salt and freshly ground pepper, to taste

1. In a medium saucepan, over high, boil the vinegar, wine and shallots until reduced by half, about 1 minute. Remove from heat and cool to lukewarm.

2. With a wire whisk, briskly beat egg yolks into wine mixture. Place over low heat and gradually pour in the melted butter, continually stirring until the sauce thickens. Salt and pepper to taste. Serve immediately.

1 1/4 cups

Filet Mignon
With Balsamic and Black Olive Glaze

Executive Chef Laurie Paul and Chef de Cuisine Tim Barrette, of San Juan Island's Friday Harbor House, developed this recipe after a trip to the beautiful city of Venice. The intensely rich sauce would be an excellent accompaniment for any steak.

BALSAMIC AND BLACK OLIVE GLAZE (recipe follows)
1 (24-ounce) beef tenderloin, at room temperature
2 onions, thinly sliced

1. Prepare Balsamic and Black Olive Glaze following directions.

2. Trim tenderloin, removing fat and silver membrane. Cut meat into four 8-ounce steaks.

3. In a frying pan, over medium-low heat, cook onions until golden and caramelized, about 20 to 25 minutes. Cover to keep warm while cooking steaks.

4. Preheat grill on high until the metal surface is very hot, so meat is immediately seared and marked. Place steak on grill and close lid. Reduce heat to medium and grill steak.

5. Use tongs when turning steak and only turn once. Cooking time will vary according to the thickness of the steak. (For a 1-inch thick steak, total cooking time should be about 10 minutes for rare.) Remember, the steak will continue to cook after it is removed from grill. It is best to remove meat from heat source before you consider it done.

6. Transfer steaks to heated plates and top with caramelized onions. Ladle sauce over onions, distributing olives evenly.   4 servings

BALSAMIC AND BLACK OLIVE GLAZE

Glaze can be made ahead. Refrigerate and reheat over low heat before using.

 ½ cup balsamic vinegar
 ½ cup Chianti Classico or dry red wine
 1 cup demi-glacé* or
     1 (16-ounce) can beef stock, reduced by half
 1 sprig fresh rosemary
 1 sprig fresh thyme
 1 sprig fresh sage
 ¼ teaspoon freshly ground pepper
 ½ cup sliced saracena or calamata olives

1. In a small saucepan, over medium-high heat, combine vinegar and wine. Simmer and reduce liquid by half. Add remaining ingredients, except olives, and reduce by half again.

2. Using a fine sieve, strain out herbs and return liquid to pan. Add olives and heat through.   1 cup

Available at specialty food stores.

Beef Tenderloin with Porcini Sauce

For several years Paula Clancey taught cooking classes in her lovely home with a spectacular view of the San Juans. She generously shared her recipe for this succulent roast and its rich, complex sauce.

PORCINI SAUCE (recipe follows)
3 pounds beef tenderloin, room temperature
¼ cup extra-virgin olive oil
Coarse salt and freshly ground pepper
1 tablespoon butter
1 tablespoon flour

1. Prepare Porcini Sauce following directions.

2. Preheat oven to 500°. Trim all fat from tenderloin. Rub with oil amd season with salt and pepper.

3. Place tenderloin on a rack in a roasting pan. Roast for 25 minutes, or until meat thermometer registers 130° for medium-rare meat.

4. Remove roast from oven and place on a cutting board. Reserve pan juices. Cover roast loosely with foil and let stand for 20 minutes.

5. If Porcini Sauce has been refrigerated, place in saucepan over medium heat and bring to a low simmer.

6. Prepare roux: In a small saucepan over medium-low, melt butter. Add flour, stir and cook about 3 minutes or until flour is lightly browned. Whisk pan juices into the roux. Add mixture to Porcini Sauce. Heat, stirring constantly, until mixture is thickened, about 3 minutes.

7. Slice meat and place on heated individual plates. Pour sauce over slices and serve immediately.   4-6 servings

PORCINI SAUCE

Sauce can be made 2 days ahead of time and refrigerated.

  1 to 2 ounces dried porcini mushrooms
  1 cup hot water
  1 tablespoon butter
  1 shallot, finely minced
  ½ cup dry red wine
  1 bay leaf
  1 sprig thyme
  1 sprig parsley
  1 cup beef stock
  Salt and freshly ground pepper, to taste

1. In a medium bowl, soak mushrooms in hot water for 30 minutes. While mushrooms are soaking, in a small saucepan, over medium-low, heat butter and sauté shallot until soft. Add wine, bay leaf, thyme and parsley; boil gently until liquid is reduced to 1/4 cup.

2. Through a fine sieve lined with paper towels, strain the liquid from the porcini; set mushrooms aside. Add mushroom liquid to saucepan and reduce by half. Pour the contents of the saucepan through the sieve again to remove herbs and shallots.

3. Clean the saucepan and return the strained sauce to the pan. Add the beef stock and mushrooms to sauce; reduce to about 1 1/4 cups. Salt and pepper to taste. Serve while warm or cover and refrigerate if made ahead.

1 1/4 cups

Stuffed Cabbage Rolls (Golubsti)

Russian-born Olga Gorman tells us that this very popular Ukranian dish is served all over the former Soviet Union. The aroma of these cabbage rolls simmering in their creamy tomato sauce will fill the room and draw your guests to the table.

> 1 large head green cabbage, cored
> 1 teaspoon salt
> Filling
>> 1 slice bread
>> ¼ cup milk
>> 1 egg, beaten
>> ½ pound lean ground beef
>> 1 cup cooked white rice
>> 1 tablespoon caraway seeds
>> ½ teaspoon paprika
>> 3 cloves garlic, minced
>> 1 medium onion, minced
>> Salt and freshly ground pepper
> Sauce
>> 1 tablespoon vegetable oil
>> ½ cup chopped onion
>> 1 (14½-ounce) can diced tomatoes, including juice
>> 1 cup sour cream
>> ⅓ cup white wine
>> 1 tablespoon dried dill weed
>> Salt and freshly ground pepper, to taste
> Mashed potatoes

1. Add cabbage to a large pot of boiling salted water, reduce heat and simmer until cabbage leaves become soft, about 15-20 minutes. Drain well; set aside.

2. To prepare filling: Tear bread into small pieces and place in medium bowl. Pour in milk and egg and combine. Add the remaining filling ingredients and mix well; set aside.

3. To prepare sauce: In a large heavy bottomed pot, heat oil over medium. Add onion and sauté until softened. Stir in remaining sauce ingredients

and simmer for 5 minutes.

4. While sauce is simmering, prepare cabbage rolls. Carefully remove leaves from cabbage head; the recipe requires 8-9 leaves. To prepare rolls, place leaf on cutting board. Put 2 tablespoon of filling on the upper third of leaf. Fold the upper portion down first, then fold in the sides and then the bottom, wrapping tightly.

5. Gently place cabbage rolls into the simmering sauce; spoon some of the sauce over cabbage. Reduce heat to low, cover and cook for 40 minutes. Serve over mashed potatoes. 4-6 servings

Bush Ranch Barbecued Ribs

The Bush family on Guemes Island is famous for their herd of Black Angus. Their guests enjoy these award-winning ribs at their home overlooking Bellingham Channel and Cypress Island.

4 pounds of beef ribs, trimmed of fat
MARINADE
 ⅔ cup thinly sliced green onions
 ½ cup soy sauce
 ½ cup water
 ¼ cup sesame oil
 2½ tablespoons packed brown sugar
 1½ tablespoons toasted sesame seeds
 1 tablespoon minced garlic
 1 tablespoon minced fresh ginger root
 ½ teaspoon cayenne
 ⅛ teaspoon freshly ground pepper
¼ cup sliced green onions, garnish

1. We recommend asking your butcher to prepare the meat by cutting the ribs diagonally across the grain into 3/8 to 1/2-inch thick strips.

2. In a large bowl, combine all marinade ingredients and mix well. Add the beef slices and turn to coat; cover and refrigerate. Allow to marinate 4 to 6 hours, turning occasionally.

3. Preheat the grill to medium. Place ribs on grill and cook 5 to 6 minutes. Turn ribs, baste with marinade and cook 5 minutes more or until desired degree of doneness. Transfer ribs to a serving platter and garnish with green onions.

6 servings

Best-Ever Meat Loaf

Meat loaf is truly an all-American comfort food. A good meat loaf should be firm, juicy and well-seasoned. Hopefully you will have some leftover for sandwiches.

1 pound extra-lean ground beef
1 small onion, chopped
2 slices bread, cubed
½ cup sautéed sliced mushrooms
½ cup finely chopped red bell pepper
½ cup ketchup or chili sauce
½ tablespoon Worcestershire sauce
2 eggs, beaten
1 teaspoon dried thyme
1 teaspoon dried basil
1 teaspoon salt
¼ teaspoon freshly ground pepper

1. Preheat oven to 350°. In a large bowl, combine all ingredients.

2. Place in a loaf pan and bake for 1 hour or until cooked through. Remove from pan and place on a heated platter. Let rest for 10 minutes before slicing.   1 meat loaf

Seafood

ERIC A. KESSLER

Purse Seiner Fishing

Pan-Glazed Salmon

From the Ships Bay Oyster House on Orcas Island comes this mouth-watering salmon recipe. The unique combination of flavors reflect Chef Christian Hogle time in the Southwest. Treat yourself to a magnificent view of Eastsound and Diamond Hill while enjoying their savory fare.

GINGER RED ONION RELISH (recipe follows)
Orange Glaze
    ½ cup fresh orange juice
    ½ cup honey
    1 cup fish stock
    2 tablespoons Ancho chile powder
    2 tablespoons cumin
    1 Pasilla pepper, finely chopped
2 tablespoons oil or butter
4 (6-ounce) skinned salmon fillets

1. Prepare Ginger Red Onion Relish.

2. Prepare Orange Glaze: In a small bowl, combine glaze ingredients.

3. In a large frying pan, heat oil over medium-high. Sauté fillets about 3 minutes on each side, or until almost done. Pour glaze over salmon and continue cooking until glaze is reduced by half.

4. Divide Ginger Red Onion Relish between four serving plates. Arrange salmon fillets on relish and top with reduced glaze.   4 servings

GINGER RED ONION RELISH

    2 red onions, thinly sliced
    ½ cup lime juice (about 4 limes)
    2 tablespoons minced fresh ginger
    2 tablespoons chopped fresh cilantro
    Salt and freshly ground pepper, to taste

In a small bowl, combine all ingredients and set aside for 1 hour at room temperature. Cover and refrigerate if made ahead.   1 1/2 cups

Salmon Cakes with Lemon-Dill Sauce

Sweet red pepper, onion and celery enhance the flavor and texture of these traditional smoked salmon cakes. The zesty lemon and dill butter sauce is a perfect topping for the crispy cakes. Enjoy this entree at the Roche Harbor Restaurant while viewing the lively marina.

    2 tablespoons butter
    2 tablespoons minced shallots
    2 tablespoons minced green onions, including some green
    2 tablespoons minced celery
    2 tablespoons minced red pepper
    3 cups smoked salmon, flaked
    2 eggs, lightly beaten
    ½ cup mayonnaise
    1 teaspoon seasoned salt
    ½ teaspoon dried dill weed
    SEASONED FLOUR (recipe follows)
    2 eggs, lightly beaten
    ¼ cup milk
    2 cups Panko bread crumbs
    LEMON-DILL SAUCE (recipe follows)
    ¼ cup butter, for frying

1. In a medium frying pan, over medium-high heat, melt butter and sauté next 4 ingredients until tender-crisp. Remove from heat and set aside.

2. In a large bowl, combine vegetables with salmon, eggs, mayonnaise, salt and dill weed. Cover and refrigerate for at least 3 hours.

3. Prepare Seasoned Flour according to directions. In a small bowl, combine eggs and milk; set aside.

4. With wet hands, role 1/4 cup salmon mixture into a ball; repeat with remaining mixture. Set aside.

5. In three separate bowls, put Seasoned Flour, egg mixture and Panko. Dip salmon balls into each bowl, in order, and place on a large cookie sheet. Gently flatten them into 1/2- to 5/8-inch thick round cakes. Cover and refrigerate, if made ahead of time.

6. Prepare Lemon-Dill Sauce and keep warm over low heat.

7. In a large frying pan over medium heat, melt butter and fry cakes on both sides until golden brown. Keep warm in oven while cooking remaining cakes.

8. Spoon 1/8 cup Lemon-Dill Sauce onto center of each heated plate. Place the cakes on the plate slightly overlapping. Serve immediately.

4 servings

SEASONED FLOUR

¾ cup Panko breadcrumbs
½ cup flour
½ teaspoon kosher salt
½ teaspoon coarsely ground pepper

1. Place Panko breadcrumbs on a sheet of waxed paper. With a rolling pin, roll crumbs until half the original size.

2. In a medium bowl, combine Panko with remaining ingredients; set aside.

LEMON-DILL SAUCE

1 teaspoon minced shallots
1 fresh sprig dill, including stem
1½ cups dry white wine
1½ cups heavy cream
1-2 tablespoons unsalted butter
2 tablespoons lemon zest
2 tablespoons fresh dill weed

1. In medium saucepan, combine shallots, dill and wine. Bring to a boil, reduce heat and simmer until wine is reduced by two-thirds. Pour into a fine strainer and discard shallots and dill. Return wine sauce to pan.

2. Add cream to wine sauce and again reduce by two-thirds, or until the sauce coats the back of a spoon.

3. Before serving, whisk in butter, one tablespoon at a time until fully incorporated. Stir in lemon zest and dill weed. 2 cups

Salmon Piccata

Enjoy this classic Italian recipe with a Northwest twist at Roberto's Restaurant on San Juan Island. The lemon, caper and butter sauce married with wild salmon provides a heavenly delicacy.

6 tablespoons butter
4 (6-ounce) wild King salmon fillets, skinned
½ cup flour
1 cup dry white wine
2 lemons, juiced
6 tablespoons unsalted butter
½ cup capers
Lemon wedges, garnish

1. In a large frying pan, warm butter over medium-high heat. Lightly dust each salmon fillet with flour. Sauté fillets about 3 minutes on each side. Remove salmon from pan and set aside.

2. Drain cooking butter from frying pan. Deglaze pan with wine and lemon juice. Add capers and butter; continue cooking until butter has melted.

3. Return salmon to pan and coat with sauce; heat through.

4. Transfer salmon to heated serving plates and top with sauce. Garnish with lemon wedges.   4 servings

Salmon with Blackberry Salsa

Serve this Northwest berry salsa with almost any kind of broiled, grilled, baked or pan-fried fish.

BLACKBERRY SALSA (recipe follows)
5 tablespoons butter or margarine
3 tablespoons fresh lemon juice
2 tablespoons brown sugar
½ teaspoon red pepper flakes
2½ pounds skinned salmon fillet
Salt and freshly ground pepper

1. Prepare Blackberry Salsa following directions below.

2. Preheat broiler. In a small pan, over low, heat butter, lemon juice, sugar and pepper flakes until butter has melted. Rinse fish and pat dry. Cut salmon into 6 portions. Place on broiling pan. Brush salmon fillets with butter mixture and season with salt and pepper.

3. Broil salmon 3 inches from heat for 4 minutes, turn fillets over and brush again with butter mixture. Broil 5 minutes more or until fish flakes when tested with a fork. To serve, remove salmon fillets to heated individual plates and spoon warm Blackberry Salsa over cooked fillets.   6 servings

BLACKBERRY SALSA

2 tablespoons olive oil
4 shallots, minced
⅓ cup sugar
2½ cups fresh blackberries, cleaned
⅓ cup raspberry vinegar or red wine vinegar
3 tablespoons creme de cassis
Salt and freshly ground pepper, to taste

In a medium saucepan, over medium, heat oil and sauté shallots until lightly browned. Stir in remaining ingredients, bring to a boil. Reduce heat and simmer about 12 to 15 minutes, or until salsa is thick but still chunky. Salt and pepper to taste.   2 cups

Grilled Honey-Mustard Salmon With Basil Vinaigrette

If you are looking for hearty Italian food, LaFamiglia Ristorante in Eastsound on Orcas Island is the place for you. Patty and Raymond Brogi's restaurant has become a favorite destination for discriminating locals as well as with island visitors.

> 4 (5-ounce) skinned salmon fillets
> 2 tablespoons olive oil
> 2 tablespoons honey
> 2 tablespoons Dijon mustard
> 1 tablespoon whole-grain mustard
> Salt and freshly ground pepper, to taste
> BASIL VINAIGRETTE (recipe follows)
> 4 cups mixed greens, washed and dried
> 4 fresh basil leaves, garnish

1. Rinse fish and pat dry. Brush fillets with oil and season with salt and pepper; set aside. In a small bowl, mix honey and mustards; set aside.

2. Preheat grill to high until the metal surface is very hot, so salmon is immediately seared and marked. Lightly oil grill. Place fillets on grill and immediately reduce heat to medium.

3. Cook about 2 minutes, turn fillets and baste with honey-mustard. Continue cooking about 8 minutes more, or until fish flakes when tested with a fork. Baste with additional sauce, as desired. Cooking time will vary according to thickness of fish. (For a 1-inch thick cut, allow about 10 minutes.)

4. While fish is cooking, prepare Basil Vinaigrette according to directions; set aside.

5. To serve, place greens in the center of individual heated plates, top with salmon and spoon Basil Vinaigrette over the top. Garnish each salmon fillet with a basil leaf and serve immediately.   4 servings

BASIL VINAIGRETTE

2 tablespoons balsamic vinegar
1 to 2 tablespoons slivered fresh basil
Salt and freshly ground pepper, to taste
¼ cup extra-virgin olive oil

In a small bowl, combine all ingredients except oil. Add oil gradually, blending with a whisk.   1/3 cup

Smoked Salmon Fettucine

This eye-pleasing pasta dish uses smoked or cooked salmon in a tomato-cream sauce seasoned with basil and garlic. It is a variation of the Crab Fettucine in our first book.

1 (16-ounce) package fettucine
5 tablespoons extra-virgin olive oil, divided
3 tablespoons pesto sauce
3 cloves garlic, minced
1 cup sliced mushrooms
4 Roma tomatoes, seeded and chopped
½ cup dry white wine
2 cups heavy cream
2 cups smoked salmon
1½ teaspoons dry basil
    or ¼ cup chopped fresh basil
⅓ cup chopped fresh parsley
Salt and freshly ground pepper, to taste
Parmesan cheese, garnish

1. In a large pot, cook pasta al dente, according to package directions. Drain and return to pot, add 3 tablespoons oil and pesto sauce; toss to coat. Cover to keep warm.

2. In a large frying pan, over medium, heat remaining 2 tablespoons oil and sauté garlic about 1 minute; add mushrooms and cook about 5 minutes or until golden brown. Stir in tomatoes and wine and cook about 2 to 3 minutes. Add cream and gently simmer to reduce, about 10 minutes. Do not boil.

4. Add salmon, basil and parsley to sauce and heat through to blend flavors, about 5 minutes.

5. Just before serving, salt and pepper to taste. Turn pasta onto individual heated plates and top with salmon sauce, garnish with cheese. Serve with additional Parmesan.

6 servings

Cedar-Planked Wild Salmon With Cider Sauce

Coast Salish Indians traditionally used cedar boards to cook salmon over an open fire. This adaptation is easier, and the result is equally as flavorful. Executive Chef Kevin Sykes at Rosario Resort crowns this Northwest favorite with a luxuriously smooth cider sauce. Serve the salmon with our Garlic Potatoes.

> **4 cups apple or pear cider**
> **½ cup butter**
> **GARLIC POTATOES (see page 187)**
> **1 (3-pound) skinned salmon fillet (sockeye, king or silver)**
> **1 (10 x 20 x 1-inch) clean, fresh cedar plank**
> **¼ cup olive oil**
> **1 lemon**
> **Salt and freshly ground pepper, to taste**
> **Thyme sprigs, garnish**

1. In a medium saucepan, over high heat, bring cider to a boil. Lower heat and simmer until liquid is reduced by at least two-thirds. Cider should be a thick syrup. Add butter and stir until blended. Cover to keep warm.

2. Prepare Garlic Potatoes and cover to keep warm.

3. Preheat oven to 450°. Rinse salmon and pat dry. Cut into individual serving pieces. Lightly oil one side of plank. Place salmon on oiled side of plank and brush top with oil. Season each fillet with a squeeze of lemon and salt and pepper. Bake the salmon for 10 minutes per inch of thickness or until fish flakes when tested with a fork. (Do not overcook; fish will continue to cook after it is removed from oven.)

4. To serve, portion potatoes onto heated individual plates. Cut fish into serving pieces and place next to potatoes. Top salmon with cider sauce and garnish each piece with a thyme sprig. Serve immediately.

4-6 servings

Mussels with Wine Cream Sauce

Large, plump Mediterranean mussels have become popular in the Puget Sound Area because they have a succulent, rich taste and they come from the water shiny and clean. (The smaller blue mussel generally requires more cleaning.) Buy mussels 24 hours in advance of cooking. To store, put them in a colander, set in a bowl and cover with a wet towel; refrigerate. Mussels should be cleaned and beards and barnacles removed just before cooking.

2 tablespoons butter
½ cup sliced green onions, including some green
4 shallots, chopped
½ cup chopped red bell pepper
1 teaspoon dried basil
2 cups dry white wine
1 cup heavy cream
¼ cup chopped fresh parsley
4 pounds mussels, scrubbed and debearded
Chopped fresh parsley, garnish

1. In a large stock pot, over medium, heat butter. Add onions, shallots, bell pepper and basil; sauté until vegetables are tender.

2. Add wine, cream, parsley and mussels to the pan. Cover and bring to a boil over medium-high heat. Reduce heat and simmer 5 to 10 minutes or until mussels are open and cooked. Shake the pan occasionally to redistribute mussels.

3. With a slotted spoon, ladle mussels into individual bowls. Pour broth over mussels in each bowl and garnish with chopped parsley. Serve immediately. 4 servings

Mussels Marinara

Blue-black mussels in a rich tomato sauce create a stunning entree. Serve this succulent dish with a fresh green salad and French bread for an elegant company dinner.

1 tablespoon extra-virgin olive oil
1 small onion, finely chopped
3 cloves garlic, minced
½ cup dry white wine
1 (14½-ounce) can diced tomatoes, undrained
¼ cup chopped Italian parsley
1 tablespoon dried basil
¼ teaspoon crushed red pepper
2 bay leaves
1 teaspoon salt
Freshly ground pepper
1 (16-ounce) package linguine
2 tablespoons extra-virgin olive oil
4 pounds fresh mussels, scrubbed and debearded
⅓ cup chopped fresh parsley, garnish

1. In a large stock pot, heat oil over medium. Sauté onion and garlic until tender, about 3 minutes. Add next 8 ingredients (wine through pepper), and cook about 5 minutes over medium.

2. In a large pan, cook pasta al dente, according to package directions. Drain, return to pot and add oil; toss to coat. Cover to keep warm.

3. While pasta is cooking, bring tomato mixture to a simmer. Add mussels, cover and cook until mussels open, about 10 minutes. Discard bay leaves and any unopened mussels.

4. Place pasta in individual shallow bowls. Spoon mussels and tomato sauce over pasta. Garnish with parsley and serve immediately.

4-6 servings

Oven-Roasted Garlic Mussels

We suggest cooking these mussels in your oven. However, you may prefer to add a smoky flavor by cooking them in a barbecue or smoker with wood chips. The larger Mediterranean mussels often open before they are completely cooked, so be sure to cook them a few extra minutes.

4 pounds mussels, scrubbed and debearded
¼ to ½ cup butter
4 cloves garlic, minced
2 teaspoons red pepper flakes
2 tablespoons chopped fresh parsley
½ cup dry white wine

1. Preheat oven to 400°. In a single layer, place mussels in two jelly-roll pans and place on racks in the center of the oven. Bake 5 to 7 minutes, or until mussels have opened and are cooked. Remove from oven and discard any unopened mussels.

2. While mussels are cooking, in a small saucepan over medium heat, melt butter and sauté garlic about 1 minute. Add remaining ingredients and heat through.

3. Pour sauce over mussels and return to oven for 2 to 3 minutes. To serve, place mussels into individual bowls and spoon remaining sauce over mussels. Serve immediately.   4 servings

Pacific Rim Mussels

Turtleback Farm Inn on Orcas Island is owned by innkeepers Susan and Bill Fletcher. They use Lopez or Penn Cove mussels to prepare this exquite blend of Southeast Asian flavor with Pacific Northwest fare.

    3 tablespoons olive oil
    ½ teaspoon sesame oil
    ½ cup thinly sliced green onions
    1 teaspoon minced shallots
    1 tablespoon minced fresh ginger
    1 teaspoon curry powder
    1 teaspoon chili powder
    1 teaspoon cayenne pepper
    1 cup dry white wine
    3 dozen mussels, debearded and scrubbed
    1 (14-ounce) can unsweetened coconut milk
    2 tablespoons chopped fresh parsley
    3 tablespoons chopped fresh basil

1. In a large stock pot, over medium-low, heat olive and sesame oils. Add green onions, shallots and ginger; sauté until onions are tender.

2. Turn heat to high, add seasonings and wine and bring to a boil. Immediately add mussels and cover. Steam until the shells open, about 5 to 7 minutes.

3. Add coconut milk, parsley and basil to mussels and heat through. When hot, spoon mussels and broth into individual bowls. Serve with crusty bread to sop up the delicious broth.   4 servings

Linguine with Lemon Clam Sauce

A simply delicious and healthy clam dish laced with lemon. For a meal in a hurry, this is the entree to choose. You will take your seat at the table less than thirty minutes from walking in the door and reaching for the pasta pot.

1 (16-ounce) package linguine
5 tablespoons extra-virgin olive oil, divided
3 tablespoons basil pesto sauce
4 cloves garlic, minced
1½ teaspoons dried oregano
½ teaspoon red pepper flakes
2 cups minced fresh clams, including nectar
    or 2 (6½-ounce) cans chopped clams
½ cup freshly squeezed lemon juice
½ cup chopped fresh Italian parsley
Salt and freshly ground pepper, to taste
⅓ cup freshly grated Parmesan cheese

1. In a large pot, cook pasta al dente, according to package directions. Drain and return to pot, add 2 tablespoons of the oil and the pesto; toss to coat. Cover to keep warm.

2. While pasta is cooking, in a large frying pan, over medium, heat remaining 3 tablespoons oil. Sauté garlic, oregano and red pepper flakes about 1 minute. Add clams, lemon juice and parsley and simmer until clams are cooked, about 5 minutes. (If using canned clams, simmer about 3 minutes.) Be careful not to over cook the clams.

3. Just before serving, salt and pepper to taste. Turn pasta onto individual heated plates and top with clam sauce and sprinkle with cheese. Serve with additional Parmesan.

6 servings

Tequila Clams

The beautifully restored Victorian Orcas Hotel overlooks the Orcas Island ferry landing. The charming hotel and lovely gardens are surrounded by a white picket fence. The food is as exceptional as are the surroundings. These delicious clams can be served as an appetizer or entree.

4 tablespoons butter
½ cup chopped onion
1 tablespoon minced fresh garlic
¼ cup diced tomatoes
1 tablespoon chopped cilantro
¼ cup Tequila
60 steamer clams (Manila or other littleneck clams), scrubbed and rinsed
    (Be sure there are no "mudders.")
1 cup water
½ lime
¼ cup sliced green onions, garnish
Lime wedges, garnish

1. In a large frying pan, over medium heat, melt butter and sauté onion, garlic, tomatoes and cilantro until onions are lightly golden.

2. Add tequila to frying pan. Keep area clear and use caution. Ignite tequila; it will flame up in a flash.

4. When flames subside, add the clams and water. Cover and steam about 10 minutes. Discard any clams that don't open.

3. To serve, divide clams and sauce among 4 bowls. Squeeze fresh lime juice over each serving. Garnish with onions and additional lime wedges.

4 servings

San Juan Island Clams in Cream Sauce

Enjoy watching the marine activity while dining at The Place Next to the San Juan Ferry Cafe. Chef Steve Anderson serves this beautiful presentation of an island classic.

½ cup butter
¼ cup chopped fresh garlic
¼ teaspoon red pepper flakes
½ teaspoon dried thyme
1 cup dry white wine
¼ cup fresh lemon juice
2 cups heavy cream
48 steamer clams (Manila or other littleneck clams), scrubbed and rinsed
1½ pounds linguine pasta
3 tablespoons olive oil
¼ cup chopped fresh basil
1 tablespoon chopped fresh parsley
1 Roma tomato, diced, garnish
1 tablespoon sliced green onion, garnish
Lemon wedges

1. In a large frying pan, over medium heat, melt butter and sauté garlic, pepper flakes and thyme for 2 minutes. Do not brown garlic. Add wine and lemon juice; increase heat to high and boil for 1 to 2 minutes. Add cream, return to boil and immediately reduce heat to a low simmer.

2. Add clams and cook until clams have opened, about 10 minutes. Discard any clams that don't open.

3. While the clams are cooking, in a large pot, cook pasta al dente, according to package directions. Drain and return to pot, toss with oil and cover to keep warm.

4. With a slotted spoon, remove cooked clams from sauce and place in a bowl; cover to keep warm. Reduce sauce until it is just thick enough to coat the back of a spoon. Stir in basil and parsley. Return clams to sauce and heat through.

5. Turn pasta into individual pasta bowls. Place clams in a circle around the

pasta. Pour sauce over pasta and clams, garnish with tomato, onion and a lemon wedge. Serve immediately.   4 servings

Ships Bay Baked Oysters

Chef Christian Hogle, of Ships Bay Oyster House on Orcas Island, developed this recipe for owner David Andrews who wanted to add a crusty baked oyster to the restaurant's eclectic repetoire. This is the place to enjoy the sunset with your dinner.

    2 lemons
    1 pound butter, at room temperature
    1 teaspoon Old Bay Seasoning
    1 teaspoon freshly ground pepper
    ¼ cup Worcestershire sauce
    ⅛ cup Tabasco sauce
    1 red pepper, finely diced
    1 green pepper, finely diced
    2 stalks celery, finely diced
    6 green onions, finely diced
    2 tablespoons minced fresh garlic
    ½ cup cooked chopped bacon
    ½ cup freshly grated Parmesan cheese
    1 cup dry bread crumbs
    40 fresh oysters in the shell, washed

1. Using a zester or fine grater, remove the outer rinds from lemons to make zest; set aside in small bowl. Juice lemons and add to zest.

2. In a food processor or mixing bowl, cream butter. Stir in Old Bay Seasoning, pepper, Worcestershire, Tabasco and lemon mixture. Add remaining ingredients, except breadcrumbs. Pulse or mix until solid ingredients are only partially pureed, to retain texture.

3. Preheat oven to 375°. Add breadcrumbs to processor and pulse again.

4. The oysters can be baked on the half shell on a bed of rock salt or shucked and placed on a baking sheet. Top each oyster with 2 teaspoons of topping. Bake until golden brown, about 10 minutes.   8 servings

Hangtown Fry

Recipes for this classic dish are common, but this variation is the best we've tasted.

12 small oysters
½ cup flour
½ teaspoon paprika
¼ teaspoon cayenne pepper
1 teaspoon salt
½ teaspoon pepper
1 large egg
2 cups finely crushed saltine crackers
¼ cup vegetable oil
2 tablespoons butter
8 eggs, beaten
4 strips cooked bacon, crumbled
1 tablespoon chopped fresh parsley

1. Rinse and pat dry oysters. In a small bowl, combine flour, paprika, cayenne, salt and pepper. In another small bowl, beat egg. Place cracker crumbs in a medium bowl.

2. Roll each oyster in flour mixture, dip in beaten egg and then roll in cracker crumbs. Place oysters on a sheet of waxed paper.

3. In a large frying pan, heat oil and fry oysters until golden brown on both sides, about 2 to 4 minutes. Remove from pan and drain on paper towel. Discard remaining oil in pan.

4. In same pan, over medium heat, melt butter. When butter is hot, return oysters to the pan. Pour beaten eggs over oysters. Lift up the cooked edges of egg, allowing liquid portion to flow underneath. Evenly distribute bacon and parsley over the eggs. Cook slowly, until the eggs are set. Cut into wedges and serve immediately. 4 servings

Crab and Artichoke Melt

Chef Bill Ray created this upscale variation of the traditional open-face crab sandwich. We were delighted with the savory combination of crab and artichokes seasoned with fresh herbs while having lunch at the Salmon Run Bistro in Anacortes.

¼ cup butter
1 tablespoon chopped fresh garlic
1 cup diced celery
½ cup diced red bell pepper
½ cup diced green bell pepper
½ cup diced green onions
1 tablespoon chopped fresh basil
1 teaspoon fresh dill
1 teaspoon dried thyme
¼ cup dry white wine
1 cup heavy cream
2 cups quartered artichoke hearts
1 pound fresh Dungeness crab meat
1 loaf sourdough bread, cut into 8 thick slices, toasted
1 cup grated extra-sharp cheddar cheese

1. In a frying pan, over medium heat, melt butter and sauté next 5 ingredients (garlic through onions) until tender. Stir in herbs and wine; simmer until most of the liquid is reduced.

2. Stir in cream, artichoke hearts and crab; heat through. Preheat broiler.

3. On a baking sheet, place toast and divide crab mixture evenly over each slice. Top each portion with grated cheese. Broil until cheese melts and bubbles. Serve immediately.   4 servings

Brewhouse Crab Cakes
With Tri-Mustard Cream

Proprietor Linda Spicher shared the recipe for these delicate, mouth-watering cakes that are a favorite entree at the Anacortes Brewhouse. A true Northwest classic.

½ pound (2 cups) cooked Dungeness crab meat
1 finely diced red bell pepper
¼ cup mayonnaise
1 teaspoon Old Bay Seasoning
1 large clove garlic, minced
1 cup flour
2 eggs, beaten
2 cups Panko (Japanese bread crumbs)
TRI-MUSTARD CREAM (recipe follows)
Olive oil or clarified butter

1. In a colander, drain the crab meat to remove excess moisture. In a large bowl, combine crab meat, red pepper, mayonnaise, Old Bay Seasoning and garlic, until mixture clings together. (It may be necessary to add additional mayonnaise to help cakes hold together.) Refrigerate for 15 to 30 minutes.

2. In three separate bowls, put flour, eggs and Panko. Form crab mixture into 8 cakes. Dip cakes into each bowl, in order, and place on large plate or cookie sheet. Cover and refrigerate, if made ahead of time.

3. Prepare Tri-Mustard Cream according to directions; cover to keep warm.

4. In a large frying pan, over medium, heat oil or butter. Fry cakes until golden-brown on each side, about 3 minutes per side.

5. Transfer 2 cakes to each heated plate and drizzle with heated Tri-Mustard Cream.

8 crab cakes

TRI-MUSTARD CREAM

1 cup heavy cream
1 teaspoon whole-grain mustard
1 teaspoon Dijon mustard
1 teaspoon prepared mustard
Salt, to taste

In a saucepan, over medium-heat, bring cream to a low simmer. Just before serving, stir in mustards and salt.   1 cup

Crab Cannelloni in Cream Sauce

Jodi Calhoun, chef at Mariella Inn, uses fresh herbs from outside her kitchen door and seafood from local waters to prepare this richly decadent dish. The Inn was beautifully restored from an early 1900s estate situated on seven waterfront acres just south of Friday Harbor on San Juan Island.

PASTA DOUGH (recipe follows)
1 (8-ounce) package cream cheese
4 tablespoons minced fresh garlic, divided
2 pounds (4 cups) fresh cooked Dungeness crab meat, divided
½ cup minced fresh basil, divided
3 cups heavy cream, divided

1. Prepare pasta dough as directed. On a lightly floured board, roll dough into a 12 x 20-inch sheet. Cut into 10 (4 x 6-inch) rectangles and set aside.

2. Preheat oven to 375°. In a food processor, combine cream cheese, 1 tablespoon garlic and 1 cup crab. Spread this mixture liberally on each of the rectangles of pasta.

3. Sprinkle the remaining crab and 1/4 cup of the basil down the middle of each rectangle. Beginning with the long side, roll each rectangle into a tube, overlap pasta slightly.

4. Pour 1 cup cream into a large baking dish. Place cannelloni seam-side down in dish.

5. Sprinkle remaining 3 tablespoons minced garlic and 1/4 cup basil over cannelloni and top with remaining 2 cups cream. Cover with foil and bake for 45 minutes. Remove foil and bake an additional 15 minutes.

6. Remove from oven and allow to rest for about 10 minutes before serving.

4 servings

PASTA DOUGH

2 cups unbleached all-purpose flour
½ teaspoon salt
3 eggs

1. Pour flour and salt into a food processor. With motor running, add eggs one at a time. Process about 15 seconds.
2. Place dough on a lightly floured board, knead until smooth. Place in a bowl and cover with a towel for 30 minutes.

Crab with Lemon Risotto

Northwest seafood pairs with traditional Italian Arborio rice in this colorful and savory dish. Prawns or scallops can be substituted for the crab.

LEMON RISOTTO (recipe follows)
3 tablespoons butter
2 cloves garlic, minced
1 cup chopped red bell pepper
2 cups cooked crab meat
⅔ cup frozen green peas, thawed
2 tablespoons fresh lemon juice
¼ cup chopped fresh parsley
Parsley sprigs, garnish

1. Prepare Lemon Risotto according to directions.

2. While risotto is cooking, in a small frying pan, melt butter over medium heat and sauté garlic and peppers until softened.

3. Place crab meat over peppers, sprinkle with peas, lemon juice and parsley. Heat through, turn off heat and cover to keep warm.

4. When risotto is done, add crab mixture and gently combine.

5. Spoon risotto onto heated individual serving plates. Garnish with parsley and serve immediately.   6 servings

LEMON RISOTTO

Zest from 1 lemon
2 or 3 lemons (½ cup lemon juice)
6 cups chicken stock
6 tablespoons butter, divided
1 cup minced onion
2 cups Arborio rice

1. Using a zester or fine grater, remove the zest from lemon; set aside. Juice the lemons and set aside.

2. In a medium saucepan, bring the chicken stock to a low simmer; keep

warm over low heat.

3. In a large, heavy-bottomed pan, melt 4 tablespoons butter over medium heat. Add onion and sauté until translucent, about 5 minutes. Stir in rice and sauté until a white spot appears in the center of the grains, about 1 minute. Add lemon juice and zest; continue stirring until liquid is absorbed.

4. Add 1/2 cup of the heated stock, and continue to stir constantly until almost all of the stock is absorbed. Repeat the procedure, adding 3/4 cup at a time, allowing the rice to absorb each addition of liquid. The intent is to allow the rice to absorb the stock a little at a time. Adjust the heat to maintain a gentle simmer; do not boil.

5. If dry, add additional broth, as needed. The risotto should be creamy and tender when done, about 25-30 minutes total cooking time.

6. Add remaining 2 tablespoons butter, salt and pepper, to taste. Remove from heat and continue with step 4 of Crab with Lemon Risotto.

8 cups

San Juan Prawn Puttanesca

Serve this spicy, piquant tomato sauce accented with prawns and artichokes over a bed of orzo or angel hair pasta.

¼ cup extra-virgin olive oil
3 large cloves garlic, minced
4 fillets of anchovies, drained & minced
¼ cup capers
½ cup chopped calamata olives
⅛ teaspoon crushed red pepper
1 tablespoon thinly sliced fresh basil or
    1 teaspoon dried basil
1 (28-ounce) can chopped tomatoes, including liquid
1 (12-ounce) package linguine pasta
2 tablespoons extra-virgin olive oil
20 medium prawns, washed and deveined
1 (5-ounce) jar marinated artichoke hearts, drained and sliced
⅓ cup chopped fresh Italian parsley
⅓ cup freshly grated Parmesan cheese, garnish

1. In a large frying pan, over medium, heat oil and lightly sauté garlic. Add next 6 ingredients (anchovies through tomatoes). Increase heat and bring mixture to a slow boil. Reduce heat, and simmer about 10 minutes.

2. While sauce is simmering, in a large pot, cook pasta al dente, according to package directions. Drain, return to pot and add oil; toss to coat. Cover to keep warm.

3. Add prawns and artichokes to tomato sauce. Simmer until prawns have turned pink on all sides about 5 minutes. (Do not overcook.) Gently stir in parsley.

4. Add sauce to linguine and toss to coat. Serve in heated individual pasta bowls. Garnish with Parmesan.

                                                  4 servings

Sautéed Shrimp with Red Pepper Sauce

This light and lively red pepper sauce complements the firm, sweet flavor of our local shrimp.

2 tablespoons extra-virgin olive oil
½ cup chopped sweet onion
2 medium red bell peppers, chopped
2 medium cloves garlic, minced
1 teaspoon basil
½ teaspoon red pepper flakes
1 (15-ounce) can diced tomatoes, including juice
2 tablespoons tomato paste
¼ cup dry white wine
2 tablespoons butter
1 pound large shrimp, peeled and deveined
1 clove garlic, minced
1 cup crumbled feta cheese
¼ cup coarsely chopped Italian parsley

1. In a medium saucepan, over medium, heat oil and sauté onion, red pepper, garlic, basil and pepper flakes until vegetables are tender. Add tomatoes, tomato paste and wine. Simmer until sauce is slightly thickened, about 15 minutes.

2. Preheat oven to 350°. While sauce is cooking, rinse prawns and pat dry. In a medium frying pan, over medium, heat butter and sauté shrimp and garlic until shrimp are just pink. Do not completely cook. (They will finish cooking in the oven. If overcooked, they will become tough.)

3. Spoon sauce into a large shallow baking dish. Arrange shrimp over the top of sauce and sprinkle with feta. Bake for 15 minutes or until cheese has melted.

4. Remove from oven and sprinkle with parsley. Serve immediately.

4 servings

Scallops and Prawns with Angel Hair

Rosario Resort has found a chef, Kevin Sykes, equal to the spectacular setting. We encourage you to visit the restaurant and enjoy his outstanding offerings. Rosario is located on 30 waterfront acres surrounding a mansion built by shipbuilder Robert Moran. The mansion, overlooking Cascade Bay, has recently been restored to its original splendor.

12 large prawns, washed and deveined
12 large scallops, washed
2 tablespoons extra-virgin olive oil
4 cloves garlic, chopped
2 shallots, chopped
2 teaspoons dried oregano
1 tablespoon lemon zest
16 ounces prepared marinara sauce
¼ cup chopped fresh oregano
1 (24-ounce) package angel hair pasta
4 tablespoons butter
1 tablespoon freshly chopped parsley
Oregano sprigs, garnish

1. Rinse prawns and scallops and pat dry. Butterfly each prawn by making an incision down the length of the back, nearly all the way through the prawn. Leave the tail attached.

2. In a large bowl, combine next 5 ingredients (oil through lemon zest). Add prawns and scallops and toss to coat. Marinate for at least 1 hour.

3. Place marinara sauce in a pan over medium heat and bring sauce to a low simmer. Add oregano to taste. Cover and reduce heat; keep warm.

4. Preheat grill on high until metal surface is very hot, so prawns and scallops are immediately seared and marked. Lightly oil grill. Place seafood on grill; close lid and immediately reduce heat to medium. Cook, turning seafood once, until the prawns have turned pink. Cooking time will vary according to thickness. Transfer to heated bowl and cover to keep warm.

5. In a large pot, cook pasta al dente according to package directions, drain and return to pot. Add butter and parsley; toss to coat.

6. Spoon marinara sauce into center of heated individual plates, creating a pool of sauce.

7. Using a large fork, twirl one-fourth of the pasta and place on top of marinara sauce. Repeat procedure to top remaining plates.

8. Arrange grilled seafood around pasta and garnish with a sprig of fresh oregano. Serve immediately. 4 servings

Penne con Calamari al Greco

Bella Isola Ristorante in Anacortes has become a favorite stop for Mediterranean food lovers. The aroma of roasted garlic and exotic spices fill the air in this warm and inviting restaurant.

10 ounces uncooked penne noodles
¼ cup extra-virgin olive oil
2 tablespoons thinly sliced fresh garlic
½ cup sun-dried tomatoes, coarsely chopped
½ cup sliced pitted calamata olives
⅛ teaspoon crushed red pepper flakes
2 tablespoons chopped fresh oregano
½ bunch stemmed spinach, chiffonade*
10 ounces calamari rings
2 cups crushed tomatoes in puree
1 cup feta cheese, divided

1. In a large pot, cook pasta al dente according to package directions, drain and return to pot. Add 2 tablespoons oil and toss to coat. Cover to keep warm.

2. While pasta is cooking, heat 1/4 cup oil in a large frying pan and sauté garlic, sun-dried tomatoes and olives until garlic turns golden. (Be careful not to burn.) Add pepper flakes, oregano and spinach and cook until spinach wilts.

3. Add calamari and continue cooking until rings open and become firm, about 1 to 2 minutes.

4. Stir in tomatoes, 3/4 cup feta cheese and cooked pasta; toss to coat. Divide between heated serving plates and garnish with remaining feta. Serve immediately.   4-6 servings

Roll spinach leaves into a cylinder and cut into 1/8-inch strips.

Seared Rare Tuna
With Sesame Spinach and Sticky Rice

Chef Greg Atkinson shared this recipe with Chef Jodi Calhoun when he was the consulting chef at the exquisite Mariella Inn, located on the outskirts of Friday Harbor. Choose the freshest and best quality tuna or Ahi available to make this dish a success. The fish is served rare to preserve the texture.

   2 tablespoons Wasabi powder*
   2 teaspoons water
   4 (4-inch) squares high grade tuna (4 ounces each)
   2 teaspoons kosher salt
   1 teaspoon dried ginger
   ½ cup clarified butter
   2 teaspoons sesame seeds
   ½ pound spinach, washed and steamed
   2 teaspoons sesame oil
   4 cups cooked short-grain rice
   ½ cup soy sauce

1. In a small bowl, combine Wasabi powder and water; set aside.

2. Heat a large cast-iron frying pan or wok over medium-high heat until pan is very hot. Season tuna with salt and ginger; dip in clarified butter. Sear tuna for 20 seconds on each side. Remove from pan and cover to keep warm.

3. In the same pan, over medium-high, heat remaining butter and toast sesame seeds for a few minutes. Add spinach and sesame oil; cook until spinach is slightly wilted, about 2 minutes.

4. On heated individual plates, place 1 cup cooked rice and top with spinach. Cut seared tuna into 1/8-inch slices and arrange around rice.

5. Pour 2 tablespoons soy sauce in 4 small bowls and place on each plate. Add 1/2 tablespoon Wasabi paste to each bowl (don't mix) and serve immediately.   4 servings

*Available in the Oriental section of most food markets.

Rockfish Tacos

Fish tacos have been around for years, and they have become popular in our area. They are a great way to enjoy our many varieties of rockfish. We suggest grilling the fish but you could also bake or fry it. Tomatillo Salsa can be purchased, but it is easy to make. For a different taste, try serving the tacos with our Mango Salsa or Porter's Salsa.

TOMATILLO SALSA (recipe follows)
3½ cups thinly sliced red cabbage
½ cup white vinegar
½ cup water
½ teaspoon salt
12 (8-inch) corn tortillas
2 pounds rockfish fillets (½ inch thick), skinned
2 tablespoons olive oil
Salt and freshly ground pepper, to taste
1 cup cilantro leaves
Sour cream
Lime wedges

1. Prepare Tomatillo Salsa. Serve at room temperature.

2. In a large bowl, combine cabbage, vinegar, water and salt; let stand for 30 minutes.

3. Preheat oven to 325°. Wrap tortillas in foil and bake until hot, 15 to 20 minutes.

4. Rinse fish and pat dry. Brush fillets with oil and season with salt and pepper. Preheat grill on high until the metal surface is very hot, so fish is immediately seared and marked. Place fillets on grill and close lid; immediately reduce heat to medium. Cook, turning once with tongs, until fish is opaque. (Cooking time will vary according to thickness of fish. For a 1-inch thick cut it would be about 8-10 minutes.) Transfer to a heated platter; salt and pepper, to taste. Cover to keep warm.

5. With a slotted spoon, remove cabbage from brine and place in bowl. Cut fish into bite-sized chunks and place in separate bowl.

6. Assemble tacos: Fill each tortilla with cabbage, chunks of fish, cilantro, a

dollop of sour cream and about 2 tablespoons of salsa. Squeeze lime over ingredients and fold tortillas. Serve with additonal lime wedges.

12 tacos

TOMATILLO SALSA

½ pound tomatillos, husked and rinsed*
¼ cup chopped onion
2 jalapeno chili peppers
1 tablespoon freshly squeezed lime juice
½ cup chopped fresh cilantro
Salt and freshly ground pepper, to taste

1. In a large saucepan, over high heat, boil 4 cups of water. Add tomatillos to water and cook until just soft, about 5 minutes.

2. In a colander, drain tomatillos and place in ice water. When cool, puree in a blender and place in a bowl.

3. Add remaining ingredients and adjust seasonings to taste. Cover and refrigerate if made ahead. 1 1/2 cups

Available in the produce section of most food markets.

Asian Oven-Steamed Sole

Flounder, cod or snapper can be used in this delicious ginger-flavored dish. Serve over Jasmine rice and accompany with our Stir-Fried Asparagus with Sesame Seeds for a memorable, truly exquisite meal.

4 (6-ounce) sole fillets
3 tablespoons soy sauce
⅓ cup dry white wine
1 tablespoon sesame oil
1 tablespoon sugar
¼ teaspoon chili oil or red pepper flakes
1 tablespoon chopped fresh cilantro (optional)
6 green onions, including some green, julienned
2-inch piece of ginger root, peeled and julienned
Cilantro, garnish
Lime wedges, garnish

1. Preheat oven to 375°. Rinse fish and pat dry; set aside.

2. In a small bowl, combine next 6 ingredients (soy sauce through cilantro) and set aside.

3. Sprinkle about 1/3 of onions and ginger in the bottom of a 9 x 13-inch baking pan. Place fillets in pan and sprinkle with soy sauce mixture. Top with remaining onion and ginger. Cover and allow to marinate for 15 minutes.

4. Bake, covered, for 15 minutes or until fish flakes when tested with a fork.

5. Transfer fish to heated individual plates and spoon sauce, including ginger and onion, over the top. Garnish each fillet with additional cilantro and a wedge of lime.   4 servings

Red Snapper with Thai Sauce

Dorothy Bird of Guemes Island serves this flavorful, eye-appealing fish dish over aromatic Basmati rice.

1½ pounds snapper fillets
¼ cup olive oil
½ cup chopped onion
2 cloves garlic, minced
1 tablespoon minced fresh ginger
½ pound mushrooms, sliced
½ red bell pepper, cut into ½-inch pieces
1 small zucchini, sliced
1 (14-ounce) can diced tomatoes, including juice
¼ cup raisins
½ cup pineapple juice
2 tablespoons sugar
2 tablespoons vinegar
1 tablespoon Thai fish sauce
1 tablespoon soy sauce
1 teaspoon Thai curry sauce
¼ cup water
½ teaspoon roasted chili paste

1. Rinse fillets and pat dry; set aside.

2. In a large frying pan, heat oil over medium, sauté onion, garlic, ginger until tender, about 5 minutes. Remove from pan and set aside. Add mushrooms, pepper and zucchini and sauté until vegetables are tender, about 5 minutes.

3. Return onion mixture to pan and add next 7 ingredients (tomatoes through soy sauce). In a small bowl, blend curry sauce and water; stir into vegetable mixture. Simmer sauce for 5 minutes.

4. Add fish fillets to pan, cover and simmer about 10 minutes or fish flakes with a fork. Place fish on a bed of rice, spoon vegetables and sauce over fish and serve.

4 servings

Snapper Esmeralda

The eclectic menu at the Rhododendron Cafe, located at the foot of Chuckanut Drive, features this attractive Cuban dish. The Green Sauce contrasts beautifully with the rosy-red snapper.

    Lime Marinade
- 8 cloves garlic
- 1 cup chopped fresh parsley
- ½ teaspoon oregano
- ½ teaspoon cumin
- ½ teaspoon freshly ground pepper
- 1 tablespoon salt
- 1 cup lime juice
- 2 cups olive oil

Green Sauce
- 2 tablespoons minced garlic
- ¼ cup capers
- 6 hard boiled egg yolks
- ¼ cup chopped parsley
- 1 cup toasted almonds
- ½ cup white wine vinegar
- 1½ cups olive oil

- 5 pounds red snapper, filleted and skinned
- 2 pounds red or russet potatoes, peeled, cooked and cooled
- ½ cup chopped cilantro, garnish
- 2 thinly sliced limes, garnish

1. Prepare Lime Marinade: Put all marinade ingredients, except oil, into a blender or food processor; pulse to combine. With machine running, gradually add oil; pour into a bowl and set aside.

2. Prepare Green Sauce: In the same blender or food processor, combine all sauce ingredients (garlic through vinegar) except oil. With machine running, add oil gradually; set aside.

3. Place fillets in a large bowl. Pour marinade over fish; turn to coat each fillet. Marinate 15 to 20 minutes. (Do not marinate any longer or lime juice will begin to "cook" fish.)

4. Preheat oven to 450°. While fillets are marinating, slice cooked potatoes

into thin rounds and line a large greased baking pan.

5. Remove fillets from marinade and place fillets on potato slices. Bake for 12 to 15 minutes or until fish flakes with a fork.

6. Divide pan contents into individual portions around snapper fillets and place on plates. Top snapper with reserved Green Sauce, sprinkle with cilantro and garnish with sliced limes.   10 servings

Roasted San Juan Rockfish

The cold waters of the San Juans are home to many varieties of fish. Roasting is an excellent way to prepare thicker cuts of fish, as long as some form of moisture is added to prevent it from becoming dry.

2 pounds thick-cut white fish (cod, snapper, halibut)
2 tablespoons fresh lemon juice
½ teaspoon salt
¼ teaspoon freshly ground pepper
1 tablespoon olive oil
1 medium onion, thinly sliced
2 cloves garlic, minced
½ teaspoon dried oregano
1 (15-ounce) can chopped tomatoes, including juice
½ cup coarsely chopped calamata olives
1 tablespoon capers
½ cup dry white wine
¼ cup chopped fresh parsley

1. Rinse fish and pat dry. Place in a single layer in a greased shallow roasting dish. Sprinkle with lemon juice, salt and pepper; set aside.

2. Preheat oven to 450°. In a large skillet, over medium, heat oil and sauté onion, garlic and oregano until onions are lightly browned. Add remaining ingredients and simmer for 5 minutes. Adjust seasoning to taste.

3. Spoon tomato mixture over fish and roast, uncovered, about 15 minutes or until fish flakes when tested with a fork.   4 servings

Baked Halibut with Three Citrus Fruits

Greg Atkinson, executive chef at Canlis Restaurant in Seattle and food writer for the Seattle Times, created this Northwest variation of a recipe from southern France for Mariella Inn in Friday Harbor. This dish marries halibut with refreshing citrus.

3 tablespoons extra-virgin olive oil
6 (8-ounce) halibut fillets
Salt and freshly ground pepper
2 oranges
2 limes
2 pink grapefruit
1 tablespoon sugar
1 teaspoon kosher salt
½ teaspoon freshly ground pepper

1. Preheat oven to 425°. On a jelly-roll baking sheet, drizzle olive oil over halibut fillets, turning to coat both sides.

2. Arrange the fillets skinned-side-down, 2-inches apart. Sprinkle with salt and pepper. Bake for 10 minutes. Remove from oven, cover to keep warm.

3. While halibut is baking, use a zester to remove the outer rind from each of the citrus fruits. Place zest in a bowl.

4. Release citrus slices from encasing membranes: With a very sharp knife, cut the tops and bottoms from all fruits. Cut away and discard the remaining peel and outer membrane from the fruit sections.

5. Save all juices, by holding the fruit over the bowl containing the zest. Cut out the sections of pulp, allowing them to fall into the bowl. Squeeze any juice from citrus membranes into bowl. Discard all peel and membranes.

6. Stir sugar, salt and pepper into fruit. Spoon mixture over the baked halibut fillets. Continue baking until heated through, about 3 minutes.

7. With a spatula, transfer fillets and fruit to heated individual serving plates. Drizzle remaining juices over each portion and serve.

6 servings

Stir-Fried Halibut with Asparagus

This dazzling Asian fish dish is highlighted with asparagus and red peppers in a spicy ginger sauce. We serve this over fragrant Thai Jasmine rice. A firm fish like red snapper or wild salmon can be substituted for the halibut.

2 pounds skinned halibut
1 teaspoon salt
1 teaspoons sugar
¼ cup dry white wine or sherry
¼ cup soy sauce
2½ tablespoons chili pepper sauce
2½ tablespoons Hoisin Sauce*
2 tablespoons ketchup
1 teaspoon sugar
1 teaspoon sesame oil
½ pound asparagus, trimmed and cut into ½-inch pieces
2 teaspoons cornstarch
2 tablespoons cold water
1½ tablespoons peanut oil, divided
2 tablespoons minced garlic
1½ tablespoons peeled, minced fresh ginger root
1 large red bell pepper, seeded and julienned
4 large shiitake mushrooms, stems removed and caps sliced

1. Rinse fish, pat dry and cut into 1-inch cubes. Place in a large bowl and sprinkle with salt and sugar; set aside.

2. Prepare sauce: In a small bowl, whisk together next 7 ingredients (sherry through sesame oil); set aside.

3. In a small saucepan, blanch asparagus in boiling water for 30 seconds. Drain and rinse with cold water; set aside.

4. In a small bowl, combine cornstarch and water. Pour over fish and with hands gently toss to coat.

5. In a wok, over medium-high, heat 1/2 tablespoon peanut oil and stir-fry the fish in batches. Cook each batch 4 to 5 minutes or until fish is opaque. Use additional oil, as needed. Place fish in bowl and set aside.

6. Add an additional teaspoon peanut oil and sauté garlic and ginger for

about 30 seconds. Add asparagus, peppers, mushrooms; stir-fry for 2 minutes or until vegetables are tender-crisp. Stir in soy sauce mixture and toss well. Add fish to wok and heat through.   4-6 servings

Available in Asian section of food markets.

Halibut With Warm Lemon-Caper Vinaigrette

Friday Harbor House is located on a prominent bluff overlooking San Juan Island's Friday Harbor Marina. While dining in the lovely restaurant, enjoy watching marine activities in the San Juan Channel and the view of neighboring islands. This tangy fresh lemon-caper vinaigrette is a perfect balance for the sweet tender flesh of halibut. The versatility of this sauce and the fresh, light flavors make it ideal for any seafood, such as tuna, prawns, wild salmon, mussels or clams.

LEMON-CAPER VINAIGRETTE (recipe follows)
2 pounds skinned halibut (approximately 1-inch thick), cut into 6 portions
2 tablespoons melted butter or oil
Salt and freshly ground pepper

1. Prepare Lemon-Caper Vinaigrette and keep warm.

2. Rinse fish and pat dry.

3. In a large frying pan, over medium-high heat, melt butter; do not allow to bubble. Place fish in pan, skin side down and cook until fish is partly opaque.

4. To sear other side, turn and cook 1 to 2 minutes. Turn heat down to medium-low and continue to cook until fish is opaque and fish flakes when tested with a fork. Cooking time will vary according to thickness of fish. (Do not overcook.)

5. Place halibut on individual heated plates and top with heated Lemon-Caper Vinaigrette.

6 servings

LEMON-CAPER VINAIGRETTE

Vinaigrette can be made ahead and refrigerated for up to 2 weeks.

2 medium shallots, diced
2 cloves garlic, chopped
Zest of 1 medium lemon
2 lemons, juiced
½ cup dry white wine
⅓ cup capers, with accompanying juice
¼ teaspoon freshly ground pepper
1½ cups extra-virgin olive oil
Salt, to taste

1. In a small saucepan, combine shallots, garlic, lemon zest, juice and wine. Simmer until reduced by half.

2. Add capers and pepper; boil one minute more. Remove from heat and whisk in oil and salt to taste. Serve immediately over halibut.   2 cups

Pineapple Smoked Halibut

The Ships Bay Oyster House, is located in the oldest farm house on Orcas Island. It is located a mile past Eastsound Village high on a cliff above Ship Bay, overlooking the waters of Eastsound. Roasted pineapple skins impart a smoky depth of flavor to the grilled halibut. The Pineapple Salsa makes an excellent accompaniment to ham or pork tenderloin.

> 1 pineapple
> PINEAPPLE SALSA (recipe follows)
> Hoisin Basting Sauce
>   ¼ cup Hoisin Sauce*
>   ¾ cup pineapple juice
>   1 teaspoon crushed red pepper flakes
>   1 teaspoon salt
>   1 teaspoon freshly ground pepper
> 2 pounds halibut fillet, cut into 4 servings

1. Peel pineapple and reserve skins.

2. Prepare pineapple skins for smoking: Place skins on a baking sheet and bake in 200° oven for 2 hours.

3. Prepare Pineapple Salsa at least 1 hour before serving; cover and refrigerate.

4. Prepare Hoisin Basting Sauce: In a small bowl, combine remaining ingredients, except halibut. Set aside.

5. On grill over hot coals, place dried pineapple skins; close lid. When smoky, place halibut on grill and baste with Hoisin Basting Sauce; close lid. After 6 minutes turn halibut and baste again. Cover and grill an additional 6 minutes or until fish flakes when tested with a fork.

6. Transfer grilled halibut to individual heated plates and top each serving with a scant 1/4 cup of Pineapple Salsa. Serve immediately.

4 servings

Available in Asian section of food markets.

PINEAPPLE SALSA

Use the peeled pineapple to prepare salsa.

> 1 peeled pineapple, cored and cut into ½-inch pieces (reserve skin for smoking)
> 1½ cups roasted red peppers, cut into ¼-inch pieces
> ¼ cup finely minced fresh ginger
> 1 red onion, finely diced
> ¼ cup rice wine vinegar
> ¼ cup chopped fresh cilantro
> 1 Serrano chili, finely diced
> ½ teaspoon cardamom

In a medium bowl, combine all ingredients. Cover and set aside at room temperature, for 1 hour. 3 cups

Guemes Island Seafood Gumbo

Mike Hardy of Guemes Island is known among his friends for his tasty variation of the traditional seafood gumbo. He uses fresh crab and shrimp in this delectable seafood stew. Mike suggests having all the ingredients prepared ahead of time before beginning the recipe. Gumbo is a blend of international cooking ingredients. The name is from the Congo word, *quingomgo*, meaning okra. It is a cousin to French bouillabaisse and has the Spanish influence of tomatoes, onions and sweet peppers. File powder (ground sassafras leaves) provides thickening and flavoring.

CAJUN SPICE (recipe follows)
1 pound smoked link sausage, sliced
3 tablespoons vegetable oil
2 cups chopped onions
4 cloves garlic, minced
1 cup chopped green bell pepper
½ cup chopped red bell pepper
1 cup chopped celery
¾ cup vegetable oil
1 cup all-purpose flour
6 cups chicken stock
½ pound frozen okra, trimmed and sliced (optional)
1 (6-ounce) can tomato paste
1 cup dry white or red wine
1 pound large shrimp, uncooked, cleaned and deveined
2 cups Dungeness crab meat (1 cooked crab)
2 tablespoons chopped fresh parsley
2 teaspoons file powder
4 cups cooked long-grain white rice

1. Prepare Cajun Spice according to directions.

2. In a large heavy-bottomed stockpot, over medium heat, cook sausage until done. Remove and drain on paper towels; set aside in large bowl. Discard sausage drippings. In same pot, heat 3 tablespoons oil and sauté onion and garlic until tender, about 5 minutes. Add peppers and celery; stir and cook another 10 minutes. Remove vegetables from pot and set aside.

3. Make roux: In same pot, over medium, heat 3/4 cup oil until it begins to smoke. Add flour and cook, stirring constantly, until the mixture turns a dark caramel color, about 10 to 20 minutes. Be careful not to burn roux. Add half of the reserved vegetables and stir to coat. Add remaining vegetables.

4. Stir Cajun Spice into roux and cook about 1 minute. Add chicken stock, stirring constantly until liquid begins to thicken. Stir reserved sausage into mixture. Add okra, if desired. Bring to a boil, reduce heat and cover; simmer for 15 minutes.

5. Add tomato paste and wine; stir until blended. Bring liquid to a simmer and add shrimp; cook 2 to 4 minutes until shrimp turns pink. (Do not overcook shrimp.) Stir in crab meat and parsley. Remove bay leaf and stir in file powder; heat through. Salt and pepper and adjust seasoning to taste.

6. To serve, place 1/2 cup rice in individual large soup bowls. Ladle gumbo over rice and serve immediately.   6-8 servings

CAJUN SPICE

  2 whole bay leaves
  2 teaspoons salt
  ½ teaspoon freshly ground black pepper
  ½ teaspoon white pepper
  ½ teaspoon cayenne pepper
  ½ teaspoon dried thyme
  ½ teaspoon dried oregano
  ½ teaspoon basil
  1 teaspoon ground cumin

In a small bowl, combine all ingredients and set aside.

Grilled Halibut
With Tomatoes and Sweet Peppers

A light and colorful dish that is pleasing to the palate as well as to the eye.
Serve with your favorite rice or pasta.

2 pounds skinned halibut, cut into 6 portions
¼ cup olive oil
1 medium onion, sliced
2 cloves garlic, minced
½ teaspoon red pepper flakes
1 red bell pepper, diced
1 yellow bell pepper, diced
1 (15-ounce) can diced tomatoes, drained
½ teaspoon dried thyme
½ teaspoon dried basil
¼ teaspoon saffron threads
½ cup dry white wine
Salt and freshly ground pepper, to taste
2 tablespoons olive oil
Fresh parsley sprigs or basil leaves, garnish

1. Rinse fish and pat dry. Brush fish with oil and season with salt and pepper; set aside. In a large frying pan, over medium, heat oil and sauté onion, garlic, and red pepper flakes for about 5 minutes. Stir in peppers and sauté until softened.

2. Add tomatoes, herbs, wine, salt and pepper. Cook over medium heat until liquid is almost absorbed, about 10 to 15 minutes. Cover to keep warm.

3. Preheat grill on high until the metal surface is very hot, so fish is immediately seared and marked. Oil grill and place fish on grill and close lid; immediately reduce heat to medium. Cook, turning once, until fish is opaque. Cooking time will vary according to thickness of fish. (For a 1-inch thick cut allow about 8 to 10 minutes.)

4. Spoon the tomato and pepper mixture in the center of six heated plates. Place grilled halibut on top and garnish.   6 servings

Vegetables/Side Dishes

CLAUDE STEELMAN

False Bay On San Juan Island

Fiery Broccoli

Whoever complained that broccoli was bland? This spiced up version of the "good-for-you" vegetable will add color and crispness to any meal.

2 tablespoons vegetable oil
1 cup coarsely chopped onion
2 cloves garlic, minced
1 jalapeno chili pepper, seeded and chopped
    or 1 tablespoon chili pepper sauce
1 pound broccoli, cut into florets, stalks peeled and sliced
1 teaspoon ground cumin
⅛ teaspoon ground coriander
½ teaspoon red pepper flakes
1 teaspoon salt
1 tablespoon water

1. In a wok, over medium-high, heat oil and sauté onion, garlic and chili pepper until vegetables are slightly browned, about 8 minutes.

2. Add broccoli, cumin, coriander, red pepper and salt and stir constantly until broccoli is bright green. Turn heat down to medium-low and add 1 tablespoon water; cover to steam broccoli. Cook until broccoli is tender-crisp, about 3 minutes. Add more water, if necessary.   4 servings

Stir-Fried Asparagus with Sesame Seeds

An eye-appealing stir-fry dish that is simple and quick. The asparagus is highlighted with a sweet soy sauce glaze.

2 tablespoons butter
1½ pounds asparagus, cut diagonally into 1-inch pieces
1 teaspoon sugar
1 tablespoon soy sauce
2 tablespoons sesame seeds

1. In a frying pan, over medium-high, melt butter. Add asparagus and stir-fry about 4 minutes.

2. Sprinkle asparagus with sugar and cook about 1 minute. Stir in soy sauce and sesame seeds and sauté 1 minute more. Serve immediately.

4 servings

Oven-Roasted Asparagus

This recipe could not be easier or more delicious. Roasting vegetables creates a unique, smoky flavor.

2 pounds asparagus spears, washed
¼ cup extra-virgin olive oil
Freshly ground black pepper
Salt

1. Preheat oven to 450°.

2. Snap off woody ends of asparagus and discard. Place asparagus on a baking sheet in a single layer. Brush liberally with oil and season with pepper.

3. Roast until tender, 6 to 8 minutes, depending on thickness of asparagus. Remove from oven and sprinkle with salt. Serve immediately.

4-6 servings

Harvest Corn

Islander Dixon Elder serves this unique dish with his Thanksgiving turkey. He tells us that this crunchy corn combined with creamy mashed potatoes and turkey gravy is the favorite part of his holiday meal.

2 tablespoons butter
⅓ cup slivered almonds
⅓ cup raw sunflower seeds
⅓ cup raw sesame seeds
1 tablespoon poppy seeds
4 cups frozen whole-kernel corn

1. In a large frying pan, over medium heat, melt butter and sauté almonds and sunflower seeds until lightly toasted, stirring frequently. (Be careful not to burn; they scorch easily.) Place nuts and seeds in a bowl and set aside.

2. Discard any blackened bits from pan. Add additional butter, if necessary. Add sesame and poppy seeds and lightly toast, stirring frequently. Remove from pan and add to reserved almonds and seeds.

3. Add corn to pan and sauté until liquid has evaporated and corn is hot. Just before serving, add reserved nuts and seeds to the corn. Serve immediately.   4 servings

Herb Roasted Vegetables

Serve these roasted vegetables as a colorful side dish or over couscous, polenta or penne pasta for a meatless entree. Small red potatoes and whole garlic can be marinated and roasted with the vegetables. Choose between oven-roasted or grilled. The vegetables can be used as a filling with Rosemary Focaccia for an authentic Italian panino (sandwich).

> HERB MARINADE (recipe follows)
> 1 red bell pepper, seeded and julienned
> 1 yellow bell pepper, seeded and julienned
> 2 zucchini, cut into ½-inch slices and quartered
> 2 yellow summer squash, cut into ½-inch slices and quartered
> 1 small eggplant, peeled and cut into 1-inch cubes
> 1 red onion, cut into 8 wedges
> 10 large mushrooms, cut into 4 wedges

OVEN ROASTED

1. Prepare Herb Marinade according to directions; set aside.

2. Add prepared vegetables to marinade and toss to coat. (Longer cooking vegetables, such as potatoes and carrots, should be parboiled for 4 minutes before marinating.) Cover and let stand for at least 1 hour. Preheat oven to 400°.

3. Using a slotted spoon or tongs, remove vegetables from marinade. Place in a single layer on a shallow oiled baking pan.

4. Bake for 30 to 40 minutes or until vegetables are tender. Turn vegetables frequently to brown on all sides. Transfer to heated dish and serve.

GRILLED ON BARBECUE

1. Prepare Herb Marinade, according to directions; set aside.

2. Add prepared vegetables to marinade and toss to coat. (Longer cooking vegetables, such as potatoes and carrots, should be parboiled for 4 minutes before marinating.) Cover and let stand for at least 1 hour.

3. Set grill rack about 5 inches from heat source. Preheat grill to medium heat. Using a slotted spoon or tongs, remove vegetables from marinade.

Place in an oiled grill basket.

4. Grill vegetables, turning once, for 6-8 minutes on each side or until tender. Transfer to heated dish and serve.　　　　　　　　　8 servings

HERB MARINADE

> 3 garlic cloves, minced
> 1½ teaspoons dried basil
> 1½ teaspoons dried thyme
> ½ teaspoon salt
> Freshly ground pepper
> ¼ cup balsamic vinegar
> ⅓ to ½ cup extra-virgin olive oil

In a large bowl, combine all ingredients, except oil. Add oil gradually, beating with a whisk until blended.　　　　　　　　　3/4 cup

Creamed Onions

Onions make an excellent accompaniment to roasted meats. Sautéing brings out the mild sweet flavor of the onions. Doreen Wickline's version of creamed onions has become a family favorite holiday dish.

6 tablespoons butter
3 large white onions, peeled and sliced
2 cups sliced leeks
½ cup chopped shallots
2-3 cloves garlic, chopped
2 cups pearl onions, peeled
1- 1½ cups heavy cream
Salt and white pepper, to taste
12-16 saltine crackers, crushed finely

1. In a large frying pan, over medium, heat butter and sauté next 4 ingredients until soft. Add pearl onions and increase heat to high.

2. Preheat oven to 350°. When onion juices bubble, stir in 1 cup cream and continue cooking until mixture begins to thicken. Add additional cream, as desired, and heat through. Salt and pepper to taste.

3. Pour mixture into a buttered baking dish and top with cracker crumbs. Bake, uncovered, until mixture is bubbly and topping lightly browned, about 40 minutes.

8-10 servings

Bistro Potatoes

Sharron Prosser recreated this recipe from a dish she and her husband enjoyed in a French-style bistro in Charleston, North Carolina. These potatoes are a flavorful addition to traditional holiday fare.

1 small head cauliflower, cored and broken into florets
2 tablespoons fresh lemon juice
3 teaspoons salt, divided
1 cup freshly grated Pecorino Romano cheese
1 cup light cream
5 pounds potatoes, peeled and quartered
6 large garlic cloves, peeled
½ cup butter, melted
Salt and freshly ground pepper, to taste

1. Place cauliflower in a large pot with enough water to cover; add lemon juice and 1 teaspoon salt. Cover and bring to a boil, reduce heat. Simmer until cauliflower is tender, about 10 minutes. Drain well. While still hot, puree cauliflower in a food processor. Add cheese and cream to cauliflower, blend to combine ingredients and melt cheese. Set aside.

2. Place potatoes and garlic in a large pot with enough water to cover; add remaining 2 teaspoons salt. Bring to a boil, with lid ajar. Simmer for 15 to 20 minutes, or until potatoes are tender when pierced with a fork. Drain well. While still warm, mash using a potato masher or ricer.

3. Stir cauliflower mixture and butter into the potatoes. Salt and pepper to taste and serve immediately.   8-10 servings

Roasted Potatoes with Rosemary

The creamy texture of Red LaSodas or Yellow Finns make them our favorite roasting potatoes. These potatoes are the perfect accompaniment to a leg of lamb or prime rib.

2½ pounds small new potatoes, cut in half
2 teaspoons salt
¼ cup extra-virgin olive oil
5 garlic cloves, slivered
2½ teaspoons dried rosemary or thyme, crushed
Salt and freshly ground pepper, to taste
3 tablespoons chopped fresh parsley

1. Preheat oven to 375°. In a large pot, partially cook potatoes in boiling salted water for 5 minutes. Drain well.

2. In a 9 x 13-inch pan, place potatoes in a single layer. Drizzle olive oil over the top, toss to coat potatoes. Sprinkle garlic and rosemary evenly over potatoes; season with salt and pepper.

3. Bake uncovered for 20 minutes, turning potatoes several times to brown on all sides. Remove from oven and toss with parsley. Transfer to a heated serving dish.

6 servings

Garlic Mashed Potatoes

A dish of homemade mashed potatoes is a traditional comfort food. This recipe offers a subtle and fragrant touch of garlic. Yukon Gold or Yellow Finn potatoes are a good choice for this dish.

> 3 pounds potatoes, peeled and quartered
> 4 large garlic cloves, peeled
> 2 teaspoons salt
> ¼-½ cup butter
> ⅔ cup milk or light cream
> Salt and freshly ground pepper, to taste
> ¼ cup softened butter

1. Place potatoes and garlic in a large pot with enough water to cover; add 2 teaspoons salt. Bring to a boil and with lid ajar, simmer for 15 to 20 minutes, or until potatoes are tender when pierced with a fork. Drain well; cover to keep warm.

2. While potatoes and garlic are cooking, in a small saucepan over medium, combine butter and cream. Heat until butter has melted.

3. Mash potatoes and garlic until no lumps remain, using a masher, ricer or electric mixer.

4. Stir heated cream and butter mixture into the potatoes. Salt and pepper to taste. Transfer to a heated serving bowl and serve with additional butter.

6 servings

Sweet Potato Gnocchi

Traditionally gnocchi are made with white potatoes, but we had these small potato dumplings at Tulio's Ristorante, in Seattle, and thought they were so wonderful we would try to duplicate their recipe. Gnocchi can be served with marinara sauce or pesto, but we favor this creamy sage-flavored sauce.

1 pound sweet potatoes, peeled
1 egg yolk, beaten
Dash of nutmeg
¼ teaspoon salt
⅛ teaspoon white pepper
1 cup unbleached white flour
¼ cup butter
6 fresh sage leaves
½ cup light or heavy cream
Salt and white pepper, to taste
Sage leaves, garnish

1. In a saucepan, cook potatoes in boiling salted water until tender, about 20 minutes. Drain the potatoes and return to saucepan. Shake the pan over low heat to remove any remaining moisture, 10-15 seconds.

2. Mash potatoes using a potato masher. (Do not use an electric mixer, it would make the potatoes too smooth.)

3. With a wooden spoon, mix in the beaten egg yolk, nutmeg, salt and pepper. Stir in flour, a little at a time, until a soft, smooth dough is formed.

4. Shape dough: Flour hands and divide dough into about 6 pieces. On a floured surface shape each piece of dough into a 1-inch rope. Cut the rope into 3/4-inch lengths. Make an indent with your index finger into each gnocchi. (This impression holds the sauce in the gnocchi.)

5. Fill a large pot with water and bring to a boil. Cook gnocchi a few at a time. When they are done, they will rise to the surface. With a slotted spoon, remove from water and place in a bowl. Repeat procedure until all the gnocchi are cooked.

6. In a medium frying pan, over medium-high, heat butter until lightly browned. Add sage and gnocchi, sauté until lightly golden. With a slotted

spoon, remove gnocchi to a heated serving dish.

7. Stir cream into remaining butter and sage in pan and heat through. Pour sauce over gnocchi, garnish with additional sage and serve immediately.

4 servings

Yams with Orange Butter

Paula Clancey combines yams with the essence of orange and freshly grated nutmeg. The effect is delicious but subtle. This dish makes an excellent fall or winter vegetable.

1 pound yams, peeled
5 tablespoons softened butter, divided
2 tablespoons minced orange zest (1 medium orange)
1 tablespoon sugar
1 medium orange, juiced
Freshly grated nutmeg, to taste
Salt and freshly ground white pepper, to taste

1. In a food processor or by hand, grate yams and set aside. In a small bowl, blend 3 tablespoons softened butter, orange zest and sugar; set aside.

2. In a medium frying pan, over medium-low heat, melt remaining 2 tablespoons butter and sauté grated yams. As the yams begin to soften, add the butter and orange mixture; stir and heat through.

3. Stir orange juice into yam mixture; add seasonings to taste. Continue cooking until yams are soft, but firm enough to hold their shape and juice has been absorbed. Transfer to a heated serving bowl.   4 servings

Potato Latkes

These crispy pancakes make a delicious accompaniment to a meat entree.

2 pounds russet potatoes
1 medium onion
¼ cup all-purpose flour
¾ teaspoon baking powder
1 teaspoon salt
¼ teaspoon freshly ground pepper
2 eggs, beaten
2 tablespoons vegetable oil
Sour cream
Applesauce

1. Grate potatoes using the shredding blade of food processor or a hand grater, transfer to a colander; let drain for 15 minutes. Grate onion and place in a large bowl; set aside.

2. Rinse potatoes with cold water to remove red-colored starch. Squeeze out excess water.

3. Add potatoes to grated onions and stir in flour, baking powder, salt and pepper; toss to coat. Stir in beaten eggs.

4. In a large frying pan, over medium-high, heat oil. Drop 1 large table-spoon potato mixture into pan for each latke. Fry until golden brown on both sides. Press latkes flat with a spatula when you turn them. Add more oil as needed.

5. Remove from pan and drain on paper towels. (Keep warm in oven, if desired.) Transfer to heated serving platter. Serve latkes with sour cream or freshly made warm applesauce.

6 servings

Classic Risotto

Risotto is a traditional rice dish of northern Italy. It should only be made with Italian Arborio rice, which can absorb liquid without becoming mushy. Perfectly made risotto is quite creamy and flows easily off a spoon. The key to good risotto is constant stirring. If it cooks too fast and becomes dry, stir in more liquid. We love it served with our braised Island Lamb Shanks.

½ teaspoon saffron threads, crumbled
6 cups chicken stock
6 tablespoons butter, divided
1 cup minced onion
2 cups Arborio rice
½ cup dry white wine
1 cup freshly grated Parmesan cheese

1. In a small bowl, combine saffron with 2 tablespoons warm water. Set aside to soak.

2. In a medium saucepan, bring the stock to a low simmer; keep warm over low heat.

3. In a large, heavy-bottomed pan, melt 4 tablespoons butter over medium heat. Add onion and sauté until translucent, about 5 minutes. Stir in rice and sauté until a white spot appears in the center of the grains, about 1 minute. Add wine and continue stirring until it is absorbed.

4. Add 1/2 cup of the heated stock, and continue to stir constantly until almost all of the stock is absorbed. Repeat the procedure, adding 3/4 cup at a time, allowing the rice to absorb each addition of liquid. The intent is to allow the rice to absorb the stock a little at a time. Adjust the heat to maintain a gentle simmer; do not boil.

5. If dry, add additional broth, as needed. The risotto should be creamy and tender when done, about 25-30 minutes, total cooking time.

6. Add the saffron, including liquid, the remaining 2 tablespoons butter and the cheese; mix well. Add salt and pepper, to taste. Remove from heat and serve immediately.   4-6 servings

Chanterelle Risotto Cakes

The trumpet-shaped, mild-flavored chanterelle mushroom grows wild in the Northwest from June through November, when there is sufficient moisture. Although expensive, they can be found in your local grocery store; be sure to give them a try. The Bay Cafe's Chef Robert Wood says of this recipe, "People love the contrast of the crunch and crusty exterior with the creamy interior of these risotto cakes." They make an elegant side dish for grilled shrimp or filet mignon.

3 tablespoons olive oil
3 tablespoons unsalted butter
1 bunch green onions, minced
2 cloves garlic, minced
½ pound golden chanterelles, cleaned with a damp cloth and thinly sliced
1½ cups Arborio rice
5 cups chicken stock
½ cup dry white wine
2 tablespoons chopped fresh parsley
½ cup shredded Parmesan cheese
1 teaspoon salt
½ teaspoon freshly ground pepper
1 tablespoon butter
Shredded Parmesan, garnish
Fresh spinach, cut into chiffonade, garnish
Toasted pine nuts, garnish

1. In a large heavy bottom frying pan, over medium, heat the olive oil and butter. Sauté the onion and garlic for about 3 minutes. Add the chanterelles and sauté until the mushrooms have released their juices, about 5 minutes.

2. Add the rice to the frying pan and cook until the rice has turn opaque.

3. In a sauce pan, over medium-high, combine the chicken stock, wine and parsley; bring to a low simmer.

4. Add 1 cup stock mixture to the rice in the frying pan and continue to stir until almost all of the stock is absorbed. Repeat the procedure 1 cup at a time until all the stock has been absorbed. Remove the risotto from the

heat and stir in Parmesan cheese, salt and pepper. Allow mixture to cool completely before forming into cakes.

5. Using a half-cup measure, portion the cakes and place onto a plastic wrap-lined pan. Refrigerate for at least two hours before the final cooking.

6. Preheat oven to 200°. In a large non-stick frying pan, over medium, heat 1 tablespoon butter. When the butter begins to foam, place the cakes into the pan in a single layer; do not crowd. Cook on one side for 3-4 minutes. Turn the cakes over and brown the remaining side. You will need to cook the cakes in batches. (The cakes should be completely browned, crusty and caramelized on each side. If this is not the case, increase the temperature under the pan.) Transfer cooked cakes to a plate and keep warm in the oven.

7. To serve, place cakes on individual plates and garnish with spinach and pine nuts.

6-8 servings

Five-Spice Basmati Rice

India's premium-quality Basmati rice is used in this spicy gold pilaf, dressed up with nuts and raisins.

½ teaspoon saffron threads
2 tablespoons warm water
2 cups Basmati rice
1 tablespoon vegetable oil
1-inch cinnamon stick
4 cloves
1 teaspoon mustard seeds
4 cardamom pods, lightly crushed
⅓ cup sliced almonds
⅓ cup golden raisins
3¼ cups water
1½ teaspoons salt

1. In a small bowl, combine saffron with 2 tablespoons warm water. Set aside to soak.

2. Rinse rice: Place rice in a large bowl and fill with enough water to cover. Drain water off repeatedly until it is no longer cloudy. Drain and set rice aside.

3. In a large saucepan, over medium-high, heat oil and sauté cinnamon, cloves, mustard seeds and cardamom for 1 to 2 minutes, to release their fragrance. Add rice, almonds, raisins, saffron (including liquid), water and salt.

4. Increase heat to high and bring water to a boil. Reduce heat to low, cover and simmer for 20 minutes. Turn off heat and allow rice to sit for 10 minutes. Fluff rice with a fork.   6 - 8 servings

Mike's Noodle Stir-Fry

This recipe was developed by Mike Smith of North beach on Guemes. Serve as a vegetarian dish or with teriyaki chicken, pork or beef.

½ pound Chinese egg noodles
6 tablespoons peanut oil, divided
2 teaspoons sugar
⅓-½ cup soy sauce
2 teaspoons minced fresh ginger
3 large carrots, julienned
1 large yellow onion, sliced
4 cups coarsely chopped cabbage

1. In a large pot, cook noodles al dente, according to package directions. Drain, rinse with cold water and return to the pot. Add 2 tablespoons peanut oil and toss to coat noodles. Set aside and allow to cool.

2. In a small bowl, combine sugar, soy sauce and ginger; set aside.

3. Preheat oven to 200°. In a large wok, heat 2 tablespoons oil over high heat. Stir-fry noodles until heated through. Transfer to a bowl and place in oven to keep warm. Turn off oven.

4. In the same wok, heat remaining 2 tablespoons oil over medium-high. Stir-fry carrots and onions until vegetables are tender-crisp. Add cabbage and stir-fry for 3 minutes more.

5. Pour reserved sauce over vegetable mixture in wok and stir to coat. Add noodles and toss to combine.   6 servings

Sesame and Ginger Noodles

This easy recipe offers a spicy accompaniment to our Asian recipes. It can be served warm or as a salad.

Ginger Vinaigrette
    ¼ cup soy sauce
    2 tablespoons balsamic vinegar
    2 teaspoons Chinese chili paste
    1 tablespoon minced fresh ginger root
    2 tablespoons sugar or honey
    ¼ cup sesame oil
1 pound Asian wheat noodles or angel hair pasta
½ cup toasted sesame seeds
⅓ cup chopped fresh cilantro (optional)
½ cup thinly sliced green onions, including some green
Cilantro, garnish

1. Prepare vinaigrette: In a small bowl, combine first 5 ingredients. Add oil gradually, beating with a whisk until blended.

2. In a large pot, cook noodles al dente, according to package directions. Drain and rinse with cold water. Return to pot, add reserved vinaigrette and toss gently to coat.

3. Stir in sesame seeds, green onions and cilantro. Garnish with additional cilantro leaves, if desired. Serve immediately. If using as a salad, cover and refrigerate. Bring to room temperature before serving.

8 servings

Polenta

This versatile northern Italian dish can be finished and served in a multitude of ways. Try it as an appetizer with our Porcini Sauce or as an accompaniment to a meat entree. It can stand alone as a vegetarian dish with a marinara sauce or fried and served with our Herbed Vegetables.

6½ cups water
1 teaspoon salt
2 cups coarsely ground cornmeal
4 tablespoons butter
¼ cup freshly grated Parmesan cheese
Salt and freshly ground pepper, to taste
Olive oil, as needed for finishing

1. In a saucepan, over high heat, bring water and salt to a boil. Reduce heat to a simmer and slowly add cornmeal, stirring constantly. Continue to cook over medium-low heat, stirring frequently. Cook until mixture is thick and creamy, about 15 minutes.

2. Remove from heat and stir in butter and cheese. Salt and pepper to taste.

3. Line a 9 x 13-inch baking pan or 2 round 8-inch pie pans with aluminum foil and spoon in polenta. With a spatula, spread into a smooth layer. Cover and refrigerate for at least 30 minutes, until polenta is cold and firm.

4. Invert pan on cutting board and remove foil from polenta. Cut into 12 squares. Polenta can be finished by frying, grilling or baking, at this time.

5. To fry polenta: In a large frying pan, over medium high, warm 3 tablespoons olive oil until hot. Fry polenta for about 4 minutes on each side, until heated through. Transfer to heated dish and serve.

6. To bake polenta: Preheat oven to 425°. Lightly oil a baking sheet, and arrange polenta squares on sheet without touching. Bake for 10 minutes, turn and bake for 5 minutes more. Transfer to heated dish and serve.

7. To grill polenta: Set grill rack about 5 inches from heat source. Preheat grill, to medium. Place polenta squares on oiled grill and cook 4 minutes on each side, until heated through and marked. Transfer to heated dish and serve.

12 squares

Porcini Mushroom Sauce

Exquisite, smoky-flavored Italian porcini, mushrooms long popular in Europe, are now readily available. We suggest serving this robust sauce over polenta wedges but it also pairs well with grilled steak or lamb. The sauce can be made two days ahead and refrigerated.

1-2 ounces dried porcini mushrooms*
1 tablespoon extra-virgin olive oil
2 cloves garlic, finely chopped
1 teaspoon dried thyme
1 cup dry red wine
1 cup beef broth
Salt and freshly ground pepper, to taste
Polenta (see page 197)

1. In a medium bowl, soak porcini in 1 cup warm water for 30 minutes.

2. While mushrooms are soaking, heat oil in a small saucepan over medium. Gently sauté garlic and thyme. Stir in wine and broth.

3. Using cheesecloth or a fine sieve, strain the porcini, reserving liquid. Add porcini liquid to the saucepan. Coarsely chop mushrooms and add to saucepan.

4. Gently simmer sauce for 20 minutes or until reduced and thickened. Add salt and pepper; adjust seasonings, to taste. Serve while hot; spoon over polenta wedges or meat of your choice.   2 cups

Available in fine food markets or kitchen stores.

Sweet and Sour Baked Beans

A classic side dish at any barbecue. This family favorite is always welcome at our Fourth of July parties.

10 slices cooked bacon, crumbled, or
    ½ pound smoked ham, diced
1 tablespoon vegetable oil
2 large onions, chopped
2 cloves garlic, minced
½ cup brown sugar
¼ cup molasses
½ cup cider vinegar
1 teaspoon dry mustard
2 (15-ounce) cans baked beans
1 (15-ounce) can kidney beans, rinsed and drained
1 (15-ounce) can lima beans, rinsed and drained
1 (15-ounce) can butter beans, rinsed and drained
1 (15-ounce) can garbanzo beans, rinsed and drained

1. Preheat oven to 350°. In a large heavy-bottomed pan, over medium heat, cook bacon until crisp. Remove bacon from pan and drain on paper towel. Drain bacon fat from pan and discard.

2. In same pan, over medium heat, add oil if necessary and sauté onions and garlic until tender. Add brown sugar, molasses, vinegar and mustard and bring to a boil.

3. Stir in remaining ingredients. Pour mixture into a baking dish, cover and bake for 45 minutes.
8-10 servings

Roasted Eggplant

The eggplant is roasted in the oven rather than fried providing a much lighter taste.

> 1 medium eggplant, washed
> 1 teaspoon salt
> ½ cup olive oil
> ¼-⅓ cup balsamic vinegar
> Salt and freshly ground pepper, to taste

1. Trim and discard ends from eggplant. Cut unpeeled eggplant crosswise into 1/4-inch thick slices; place on paper towels. Sprinkle eggplant with salt and let stand for about 20 minutes.

2. Preheat oven to 400°. Brush baking sheet with oil and lay eggplant slices on sheet. Oil top side of eggplant. Bake about 10 minutes or until light brown and tender, turn and bake for 5 minutes more.

3. Remove from oven and place in a shallow serving dish. While eggplant is still warm, drizzle with vinegar and season with salt and pepper. Serve at room temperature.   4 servings

Gingered Vegetables in Black Bean Sauce

This eye-appealing dish is delicious served with a traditional Asian meal or a simple meat entree.

2 tablespoons soy sauce
1 tablespoon dry sherry
2 tablespoons cornstarch
2 tablespoons water or chicken stock
2 tablespoons vegetable oil
1 large onion, julienned
2 cloves garlic, minced
1½ teaspoons fresh minced ginger
2 carrots, julienned
1½ cups cauliflower, florets
2 medium zucchini, julienned
1 red bell pepper, julienned
1 green bell pepper, julienned
2 tablespoons black bean sauce

1. In a small bowl, combine first 4 ingredients and set aside.

2. In a large frying pan or wok, over medium high, heat oil. Add onion, garlic, ginger, carrots and cauliflower. Sauté about 3 minutes.

3. Add zucchini, peppers and bean sauce and cook until tender-crisp, about 4 minutes; stirring constantly.

4. Stir in soy sauce mixture and cook until slightly thickened, about 1 minute. Transfer to a heated serving dish and serve immediately.

6 servings

Soups

Orca Spy Hopping

Manhattan Clam Chowder

There are two sides to the clam chowder debate, those who stand by the red Manhatten and those who stand by the New England or white version. While we may never be able to influence either group, we offer you this rendition of red clam chowder.

8 slices bacon, cut into 1-inch pieces
2 tablespoons olive oil
1 cup chopped onion
2 cloves garlic, minced
½ cup diced carrot
½ cup green or red bell pepper
½ cup chopped celery
3 cups diced potatoes
1 (8-ounce) bottle clam juice
1 (15-ounce) can diced tomatoes, including juice
1 teaspoon dried thyme
1 teaspoon salt
2 teaspoons Worcestershire sauce
⅛ teaspoon Tabasco sauce
½ teaspoon freshly ground pepper
2 tablespoons chopped fresh parsley
2 (6½-ounce) cans chopped clams, including juice

1. In a large stockpot, over medium-high heat, fry bacon until cooked; do not brown. Remove and drain on paper towels; set aside. Discard grease from pot.

2. In same pot, heat oil and sauté onion until tender. Add garlic and cook 2 minutes more. Add carrots, peppers, celery and potatoes; cover and cook about 5 minutes, until tender-crisp.

3. Add bottled clam juice and just enough water to cover vegetables; bring to a low simmer. Cover and simmer until vegetables are tender, about 10 minutes.

4. Add remaining ingredients and reserved bacon. Simmer, uncovered, for about 10 minutes or until heated through.   4-6 servings

Island Clam Chowder

This is the best white chowder ever! Serve this classic with garlic bread or crackers. If using canned clams, add them to the pot after vegetables are cooked. Other seafoods (shrimp, prawns, scallops) or fish can be substituted for the clams.

8 slices bacon, diced
1 tablespoon butter
1 small onion, diced
2 cloves garlic, minced
2 cups chopped fresh clams or
      2 (6½-ounce) cans chopped clams
2 (8-ounce) bottles clam nectar
1 quart water
4 medium potatoes, diced
2 carrots, sliced
2 celery stalks, chopped
½ teaspoon dried oregano
½ teaspoon dried thyme
½ teaspoon dried marjoram
¼ cup butter
3 tablespoons flour
2 cups light cream
1 cup milk
1 tablespoon chopped fresh parsley
Salt and freshly ground pepper, to taste
4 dashes Tabasco sauce

1. In a large stock pot, over medium heat, fry bacon. Remove and drain on paper towels; set aside in a medium bowl. Discard bacon drippings. In the same pot, melt butter and sauté onion and garlic until tender, about 5 minutes.

2. Push onion mixture to the side of the pot; add fresh clams and sauté lightly, about 4 minutes. Do not overcook. With a slotted spoon, remove clams and onion mixture; add to reserved bacon.

3. In same pot, combine next 8 ingredients (nectar through marjoram). Bring to a boil, reduce heat; cover and simmer until vegetables are tender. If

using canned clams, add them now.

4. Make roux: In a saucepan, over medium heat, melt butter and blend in flour until slightly brown. Gradually whisk in cream and milk. Continue cooking, stirring constantly until mixture thickens; do not boil. Slowly stir cream mixture into pot.

5. Add reserved bacon, onion mixture, clams and parsley to pot. Add salt, pepper and Tabasco; adjust seasonings to taste. Heat chowder through but do not boil. Ladle into heated bowls and serve.   6 servings

Italian Clam Soup

The Rhododendron Cafe, located in the tiny town of Bow in Skagit Valley, is a popular destination for locals and tourists alike. This aromatic, hearty soup is one sample from their eclectic menu.

2 tablespoons olive oil
1 cup diced onion
1 tablespoon minced garlic
1 cup diced celery
½ red bell pepper, diced
½ green pepper, diced
2 cups chopped artichoke hearts
1 (16-ounce) can diced tomatoes
2 pounds in the shell, manila or littleneck clams, steamed and shucked
    or 2 cups chopped cooked clams
8 cups clam juice
1 teaspoon salt
1 teaspoon pepper
1 tablespoon chopped fresh basil
1 tablespoon minced fresh oregano
3 cups diced zucchini
Salt and pepper, to taste
Parmesan cheese, garnish

1. In a large pot, over medium, heat oil and sauté onion until tender. Add garlic, celery and peppers; cook until soft. Add all other ingredients except zucchini and simmer about 10 minutes.

2. Add zucchini and cook until tender-crisp, about 4 minutes. Add salt and pepper to taste and additional seasonings, as needed. Serve in individual soup bowls. Garnish with Parmesan cheese.   8-10 servings

Thousand Flavor Soup

Proprietor and Chef Steve Anderson of The Place Next to the San Juan Ferry Cafe offers an eclectic menu featuring local produce, seafoods and meats. The restaurant is situated in the oldest building still standing in Friday Harbor and sits directly over the water. The combination of flavors is exquisite in this Thai-influenced soup.

¼ cup butter
½ cup finely chopped yellow onion
1 teaspoon chopped fresh garlic
1 teaspoon finely chopped lemongrass
½ teaspoon minced fresh ginger root
½ cup finely chopped celery
¼ cup flour
2½ cups chicken broth
2 cups whole milk
½ cup heavy cream
1 cup thinly sliced shiitake mushrooms
2 cups chopped mixed greens (baby lettuces, baby spinach, radicchio, beet greens, purple kale, mustard greens and mazula, or greens of your choice.)
2 teaspoons coarsely chopped fresh dill
2 teaspoons chopped fresh cilantro
2 teaspoons chopped fresh basil
1 tablespoon sliced green onion
1 teaspoon chopped fresh parsley
½ teaspoon lemon or lime juice
2 dashes Tabasco sauce
Salt and freshly ground white pepper

1. In a large pot, over medium heat, melt butter and sauté onion, garlic, lemongrass, ginger and celery until tender, about 4 minutes. Add flour and cook 2 minutes more, stirring constantly.

2. In a medium saucepan, over medium heat, combine broth, milk and cream; heat until hot. With a wire whisk, slowly blend broth into sautéed vegetables until completely incorporated.

3. Add remaining ingredients to pot and heat through. Salt and pepper to taste and serve immediately.   4 servings

Dungeness Crab Bisque

Historic Roche Harbor is located at the northwest end of San Juan Island. In the 1850s the hotel was a Hudson's Bay Trading Post. In the late 1800s the area was home to the largest lime quarry in the western United States. Today it is the site of a world-class resort and restaurant. This wonderfully rich soup starring locally harvested crab is the restaurant's most requested recipe. Now you can enjoy it, too, thanks to executive chef Bill Shaw.

3 tablespoons butter
⅓ cup flour
1 medium carrot, sliced
1 celery stalk, sliced
1 red bell pepper, diced
1 green bell pepper, diced
1 yellow onion, sliced
1 clove garlic, minced
2 tablespoons butter
1 tablespoon minced fresh parsley
½ tablespoon coarsely chopped chives
1 teaspoon chopped fresh tarragon
2 tablespoons brandy
2 tablespoons Spanish paprika
¼ cup Old Bay Seasoning
⅛ teaspoon cayenne pepper
¼ teaspoons freshly ground black pepper
1½ cups whole milk
2¼ cups heavy cream
1 cup Dungeness crab meat

1. In a medium saucepan, over medium heat, melt butter and whisk in flour to create a roux. Let the roux cook for 4-5 minutes stirring frequently to prevent scorching. Remove from heat and set aside.

2. In a food processor, place prepared vegetables (carrots through garlic) and process to a fine mince.

3. In a large heavy-bottomed stock pot, over medium heat, melt 2 tablespoons butter. Add minced vegetables and fresh herbs (parsley through tarragon); sauté until tender-crisp.

4. Add brandy to vegetables and deglaze pan. Add the spices and cook mixture for 3 to 4 minutes.

5. Whisk milk and cream into vegetables.

6. Cook bisque over low heat for 30-40 minutes, or until bisque is thick. Stir frequently to prevent scorching the bottom of the pot.

7. Add crab and heat through; transfer to individual heated serving bowls.

4 servings

Salmon Creole Soup

The Rhododendron Cafe, well-situated at the south end of scenic Chuckanut Drive, attracts a regular clientele with its imaginative interpretations of Northwest cuisine. This soup adds peppery topnotes to our local salmon. Serve with crusty bread, a green salad and a hearty red wine.

2 tablespoons butter
1 cup diced onion
1 tablespoon minced garlic
½ red bell pepper, diced
½ cup green bell pepper, diced
1 cup diced celery
1 tablespoon flour
2 quarts salmon stock
6 cups clam juice
1 teaspoon thyme
½ teaspoon rosemary
½ teaspoon white pepper
1 teaspoon salt
1 teaspoon freshly ground black pepper
½ teaspoon cayenne pepper
¾ cup uncooked long grain rice
4 tablespoons butter
¼ cup flour
3 cups cooked salmon pieces
Salt and freshly ground pepper, to taste

1. In a large pot, over medium, heat butter and sauté onion, garlic, bell peppers and celery until soft. Stir in flour.

2. Add salmon stock, clam juice, herbs and seasonings to vegetables; bring to a boil. Add rice; cook 10 to 15 minutes until rice is tender.

3. Prepare roux while rice is cooking. In a small saucepan, over medium heat, warm 4 tablespoons butter and blend in 1/4 cup flour. Stirring constantly, cook about 5-10 minutes or until roux is brown. Be careful not to burn. Remove from heat.

4. When rice is done, blend 1/4 cup of soup stock into roux; blend it back into soup pot. This will prevent roux from lumping in soup.

5. Add salmon to soup and heat through; do not boil. Add salt and pepper to taste and additional seasonings, as needed. Serve in individual soup bowls. 8-12 servings

Creamy Vegetable Soup

Kathy's Pies and Cakes on San Juan Island offers much more than the name implies. Kathy Mohrweiss created this healthful soup for her catering business.

2 large potatoes, peeled and quartered
1 tablespoon vegetable oil
½ large onion, chopped
8 carrots, chopped
3-4 cups vegetable stock
¼ cup tahini*(toasted sesame seed paste)
2 cups frozen corn kernels
2 cups frozen peas
Salt and freshly ground pepper, to taste

1. In a medium pot, place potatoes in enough cold water to cover. Heat to boiling, turn heat down and simmer, covered, until tender-crisp. Remove from heat, drain and cut potatoes into small cubes; set aside.

2. In a stock pot, heat oil and sauté onion and carrots about 4 minutes. Add 2 cups stock and continue cooking until carrots are tender-crisp. Add cubed potatoes and continue cooking until vegetables are tender. Remove from heat and set aside 1 1/2 cups of the vegetable mixture; puree remaining vegetables and stock.

3. Return pureed vegetables to pot; stir in remaining stock and tahini. Bring to a low simmer and add reserved vegetables, corn and peas. Heat through and season with salt and pepper. 6-8 servings

Available in most food markets.

Minestrone

This hearty Italian soup makes a perfect cold-weather meal. For the full effect, serve it with a loaf of rustic bread and a full-bodied Chianti wine.

8 slices lean bacon, diced
2 tablespoons extra-virgin olive oil
1 medium onion, chopped
2-3 cloves garlic, minced
2 celery stalks, chopped
3 carrots, peeled and sliced
3 cups finely shredded cabbage
2 large potatoes, peeled and diced
1 (28-ounce) can crushed tomatoes
¼ pound dried cannellini beans, cooked according to package directions
    or 1½ cups drained canned beans
2 small zucchini, halved lengthwise and sliced
6 cups beef or chicken stock
¼ cup chopped Italian parsley
2 teaspoons dried oregano
¼ cup fresh minced basil
    or 2 teaspoons dried basil
½ cup small shaped pasta, uncooked
Salt and freshly ground pepper, to taste
¼ cup basil pesto
Parmesan cheese, garnish

1. In a large stock pot, over medium, sauté bacon. Remove bacon and drain; set aside. Discard grease.

2. In the same pot, heat oil. Sauté onion, garlic, celery and carrots until tender-crisp, about 7 minutes. Add cabbage and potatoes and sauté an additional 4 minutes.

3. Add tomatoes, beans, zucchini, stock, reserved bacon, parsley, oregano and basil. With the lid ajar, simmer for 45 minutes.

4. Increase heat and stir in pasta. Cook pasta until al dente, according to package directions. Salt and pepper to taste.

5. Stir in pesto at the last minute. Serve in individual soup bowls. Garnish with Parmesan cheese.
8 servings

Curried Pumpkin Soup

Autumn means pumpkins in Skagit County. Georgia of Georgia Johnson's Fine Catering in La Conner created this pumpkin recipe with the help of her sister, Maggie and friend Eddie Gordon. His family owned farm has been growing winter squashes and pumpkins since 1969. The farm's pumpkin display in October brings Jack O' Lantern carvers and pumpkin lovers from all over western Washington.

2 tablespoons olive oil
2 medium yellow onions, coarsely chopped
1 teaspoon salt
½ teaspoon white pepper
2 teaspoons curry powder
2 pounds cooked pureed pumpkin or butternut squash (1 large can pumpkin puree can be substituted)
1 quart milk or light cream
Yogurt, garnish
Cinnamon, garnish

1. In a large stock pot, heat oil over medium. Add onions, salt, pepper and curry and sauté until onions are very soft and slightly caramelized. Add cooked pumpkin or squash and heat through.

2. Remove from heat and, in several batches, add the pumpkin mixture and a little milk or cream to a food processor or blender and process until smooth.

3. Pour mixture back into the soup pot. Add remaining milk or light cream and heat through.

4. Ladle into soup bowls. Garnish with a dollop of yogurt and sprinkle with cinnamon, if desired.   6-8 servings

Sweet Potato Soup with Lime Cream

Cafe Olga is located in the tiny town of Olga, located east of Moran State Park on Orcas Island. Owner and chef Marcy Lund and her staff create wholesome, sumptuous fare in her cozy cafe.

2 pounds sweet potatoes, peeled and quartered
1 cup onion, diced
4 cups chicken broth
1 jalapeno chili pepper, seeded and chopped
Salt and freshly ground pepper, to taste
Lime Cream
    ½ cup sour cream
    ½ teaspoon lime zest
    1½ tablespoons lime juice

1. In a large stock pot, combine first 4 ingredients and bring to a boil. Cover and reduce heat. Simmer until potatoes are tender. Remove from heat.

2. Place contents of stock pot in the bowl of a food processor. Pulse until ingredients are puréed. Return to stock pot and heat through. Salt and pepper to taste.

3. While soup is reheating, in a small bowl, prepare Lime Cream by combining remaining ingredients. Set aside.

4. Ladle soup into individual heated soup bowls and garnish with a dollop of Lime Cream. Serve immediately.   4-6 servings

Eggplant Soup

This soup comes with high accolades from Anne McCracken of North Beach. She says, "This is the best hearty soup I have ever eaten."

1 pound bulk sweet Italian sausage
6 tablespoons extra-virgin olive oil, divided
4½ cups cubed (½-inch) unpeeled eggplant
1½ teaspoons salt, divided
1½ cups chopped onion
½ cup chopped fennel bulb or celery
2 tablespoons minced garlic
2 teaspoons ground or crushed fennel seed
½ teaspoon freshly ground pepper
4 bay leaves
1 teaspoon dried basil
1¼ teaspoons dried thyme
1½ cups chicken stock
1 (10-ounce) can heavy tomato puree
1 (28-ounce) can chopped peeled tomatoes, including juice
Salt and pepper, to taste

1. In a large stock pot, over medium-high, sauté sausage, breaking it into small pieces, until browned. Drain and turn onto paper towels.

2. In the same pot, over medium-high, heat 4 tablespoons oil. Add eggplant and 1/2 teaspoon salt; sauté, stirring occasionally, for about 4 to 5 minutes. Transfer eggplant to bowl and set aside.

3. In the same pot, over medium-high, add remaining 2 tablespoons oil, onion, fennel, garlic, fennel seed, pepper, bay leaves, remaining 1 teaspoon salt, basil and thyme. Sauté until onion is tender, about 5 minutes.

4. Add reserved sausage, eggplant and remaining ingredients. Cover and simmer about 10 to 15 minutes. Thin with additional chicken stock if soup seems too thick; add additional seasoning as desired. Remove bay leaves before serving.   6-8 servings

Friday Harbor Black Bean Chili

The Front Street Cafe, overlooking the San Juan Island ferry terminal in Friday Harbor, serves this full-bodied vegetarian chili with Jalapeno Beer Cornbread. It is a perfect combination to warm you up on a blustery Northwest day.

2 cups dry black beans
1 (15-ounce) can diced tomatoes, including juice
1 (7-ounce) can diced green chilies
2 tablespoons dried cumin
2 tablespoons chili powder
2 tablespoons dried oregano
2 tablespoons dried basil
½ tablespoon minced garlic
1 teaspoon salt
1 teaspoon freshly ground pepper
Jalapeno Beer Cornbread, (see page 245)

1. In a colander, sort and rinse dry beans. Place beans in a large stockpot, add cold water to cover. Soak beans overnight.

2. Drain beans and return to stockpot with enough fresh water to measure 2 inches above beans. Over high heat, bring beans to a boil. Reduce heat to low and simmer, with lid ajar, about 1 1/2 hours. Stir occasionally, to prevent sticking. The beans will begin to crack when they are tender. (Test periodically to see if they are done.)

3. Add all remaining ingredients and simmer on low heat for 1 hour. Adjust seasonings to taste.   8-10 servings

Greek Lentil Soup

This hearty, vegetarian soup is served at Calico Cupboard Cafe and Bakery. The first Calico Cupboard opened in LaConner 16 years ago. Because of its popularity with both locals and tourists there are now restaurants in Anacortes and Mt. Vernon.

2 cups brown lentils, washed
8 cups vegetable broth
1½ teaspoons whole coriander seed
1 teaspoon dried oregano
1 teaspoon dried basil
½ teaspoon dried thyme
1 teaspoon ground bay leaf
1½ teaspoons olive oil
2 teaspoons minced garlic
1 large onion, diced
1½ teaspoons finely chopped jalapeno chili pepper
2 medium potatoes, scrubbed and diced
4 ribs celery, diced
2 cups peeled and chopped butternut squash
1 package frozen chopped spinach, thawed
¼ cup lemon juice
1 teaspoon salt
Freshly ground pepper, to taste

1. Spray stock pot with vegetable spray. Add lentils and vegetable broth and bring to a boil. Add herb seasonings and continue to cook over medium heat until lentils are tender, about 20 minutes.

2. In a small frying pan, over medium, heat olive oil. Sauté garlic and onion until translucent; add to stock pot.

3. To the stock pot add jalapeno, potato, celery and squash. Cook until tender, about 10 minutes. Add spinach and lemon juice; heat through. Salt and pepper to taste. Transfer to individual soup bowls and serve.

8-10 servings

Breakfasts/Breads

KATHLEEN BROWN   *Sucia Island*

Northwest Eggs

This recipe comes to us from Susan Fletcher of Turtleback Farm Inn, on Orcas Island. The Inn overlooks eighty acres of forest and farmland in beautiful Crow Valley. This dish, typical of the extraordinary breakfasts served by Susan and her husband Bill, can be served as a gourmet breakfast or a light dinner. Local Dungeness crab can be substituted for the salmon.

    5 eggs
    1 ½ cups milk
    1 teaspoon Dijon mustard
    1 teaspoon fresh lemon juice
    4 ounces cream cheese
    2 tablespoons sour cream
    ½ teaspoon dill weed
    2 teaspoons capers
    8 ounces smoked salmon, crumbled
    Sour cream, garnish
    Capers, garnish
    Dill weed, garnish

1. Preheat oven to 375°. In a blender, combine first 7 ingredients (eggs through dill weed) and blend. With a spoon, stir in capers and salmon.

2. Pour mixture into a buttered 10-inch pie dish. Bake for 40 minutes or until puffed and lightly browned. Remove from oven and allow to set for 5 minutes.

3. Cut into eight slices and transfer to heated individual serving plates. Garnish each slice with a dollop of sour cream, a few capers and a sprig of fresh dill. Serve with muffins or biscuits. 8 servings

Breakfast Wraps

The Star Bar in old town Anacortes is owned and operated by Sandy and James Harper, a mother-and-son team of food-loving world travelers. The cozy vegetarian cafe serves fresh juices and huge, healthy burritos called "wraps." Ethnic ingredients rolled up in chapatis are dished out in a spirit of fun and friendliness.

1 (12-ounce) can black beans, including liquid
1 teaspoon cumin
1 teaspoon chili powder
½ teaspoon salt
¼ teaspoon freshly ground pepper
1 tablespoon vegetable oil
½ cup thinly sliced onion
¾ cup chopped red and green bell peppers, combined
12 eggs, beaten
4 chapatis* (or 8 flour tortillas)
1 cup grated Cheddar and Jack cheese, combined
1 cup salsa
½ cup light sour cream
PICO DE GALLO (recipe follows)
¼ cup chopped green onions
Cilantro leaves, garnish

1. In a saucepan, over medium heat, combine beans and seasonings. Simmer until liquid is reduced. Remove from heat and cover to keep warm.

2. In a large frying pan, over medium, heat oil and sauté onion and peppers until tender, about 5 minutes. Stir in eggs and scramble with vegetables. Remove from heat and cover to keep warm.

3. Assemble wrap: In a large frying pan, over medium, heat chapati turning once. Sprinkle with 1/4 cup of cheese; heat until cheese is melted.

4. Remove from pan and place on a warm plate. Spoon 1/4 of the scrambled eggs, beans and salsa down the middle. Roll chapati half way, fold in ends and finish rolling.

5. Top with 1/4 of the sour cream, Pico de Gallo and green onions. Repeat procedure for remaining chapatis. Garnish with cilantro leaves and serve immediately.   4 servings

PICO DE GALLO

- 1 cup Roma tomatoes, quartered and sliced
- ½ cup chopped red and white onions, combined
- ¼ cup chopped cilantro
- 1 tablespoon olive oil
- 1 tablespoon fresh lemon juice
- 2 teaspoons red wine vinegar

In a small bowl, combine all ingredients. Cover and refrigerate, if made ahead.

1 1/2 cups

Chapatis are large vegetable-flavored tortillas, available in specialty food markets.

Potato and Egg Breakfast Casserole

Hillside House, a bed and breakfast in Friday Harbor on San Juan Island, serves this flavorful potato dish to their lucky guests. Vary the ingredients to suit your taste and the contents of your refrigerator. This casserole can be prepared the night before for a carefree breakfast.

4 pounds Russet potatoes, unpeeled
10 eggs
½ cup milk
1 cup sour cream
⅓ cup flour
½ teaspoon baking powder
¼ teaspoon garlic powder, or to taste
Salt and freshly ground pepper, to taste
2 cups shredded Cheddar cheese, divided
1 cup chopped onions
1 cup salsa
1 cup chopped tart apple
1 pound cooked bacon, crumbled

1. In a large pan, cook potatoes until tender. Cool, peel if desired and slice. Set aside.

2. In a large mixing bowl, beat eggs lightly. Mix in milk, sour cream, flour, baking powder and seasonings. Set aside.

3. Preheat oven to 350°. Grease a 9 x 13-inch baking dish. Layer bottom with 1/2 of the potato slices. Alternate with layers of 1 cup cheese, onions, salsa and apples.

4. Cover with remaining potato slices, top with remaining 1 cup cheese and bacon.

5. Pour egg mixture evenly over the top. (Casserole can be covered and refrigerated at this time.) Bake uncovered, for 1 hour, until cheese is golden brown.

6. Let casserole sit for about 15 minutes before cutting. Cut into individual servings and serve warm.   12 servings

Broccoli and Mushroom Frittata

A frittata is an open-faced omelet that is broiled. Its appeal is that you can use ingredients that you have on hand, or seasonal vegetables. Fresh asparagus, artichokes, prosciutto, crab or smoked salmon are a few suggestions for fancier fillings. A frittata is a welcome choice for brunch or a light supper.

2 cups fresh broccoli, trimmed and cut into bite-size pieces
6 eggs
½ cup freshly grated Parmesan cheese
2 tablespoons butter or margarine
¼ cup minced red onion
¾ cup sliced mushrooms
½ red bell pepper, chopped
Salt and freshly ground pepper
Chopped fresh parsley, garnish

1. In a medium saucepan, cover and steam broccoli in a small amount of salted water until tender-crisp, about 5 minutes. Drain and set aside.

2. Preheat broiler. In a large bowl, beat eggs and stir in cheese; set aside.

3. In a 12-inch flameproof frying pan, melt butter over medium heat. Sauté onions, mushrooms and peppers until tender, about 5 minutes.

4. Add reserved broccoli and distribute evenly in pan. Pour eggs over vegetables; season with salt and pepper. Reduce heat to medium-low. As eggs begin to set, lift up the cooked edges of egg, allowing liquid portion to flow underneath. Continue to cook until eggs are softly set and top is still moist.

5. Place frying pan under the broiler, about 4 inches from heat and cook until frittata is golden and sizzling, about 2 minutes.

6. Remove from broiler, cut into wedges and garnish with parsley; serve immediately.   4 servings

Potato and Pepper Sauté

This glorious combination of crispy potatoes and vegetables makes an irresistible side dish or a meal on its own. It makes a delicious breakfast entree.

2 pounds medium red potatoes
1 teaspoon salt
4 tablespoons butter
2 tablespoons olive oil
2 cloves garlic, minced
½ cup diced green bell pepper
½ cup diced red bell pepper
½ cup chopped green onions, including some green
2 tablespoons minced fresh parsley or cilantro
Salt and freshly ground pepper, to taste
2 cups grated cheddar cheese
1 avocado, peeled and sliced
1 cup sour cream
2 cups salsa

1. Prepare potatoes a day ahead. Wash potatoes and cut in half. In a large pot, cook potatoes in boiling salted water until tender but firm, about 10 minutes.

2. Drain potatoes and place in a large bowl, cover and refrigerate overnight.

3. For best results, remove potatoes from refrigerator 1 hour before preparation. Dice potatoes into 1/2-inch cubes and set aside.

4. In a large frying pan, over medium, heat butter and oil. Add potatoes, peppers, garlic, and onion and sauté until vegetables are tender and slightly brown, about 15-20 minutes. Add additional oil or butter, as needed. Gently stir in parsley. Salt and pepper, to taste.

5. Spoon onto individual heated plates; sprinkle with cheddar cheese. Broil to melt cheese, if desired. Top with avocado slices and a dollop of sour cream. Serve with a dish of salsa.   4-6 servings

Sausage and Hominy Breakfast Casserole

This is a favorite family breakfast served on special occasions. It offers all the comfort of an old-fashioned southern dish that fills the stomach as well as gladdening the heart.

    1 pound lean sausage meat
    1 tablespoon vegetable oil
    1 cup chopped onion
    1 cup chopped celery
    ½ cup diced red bell pepper
    ½ cup chopped fresh parsley
    1 beaten egg
    1 cup milk
    3 (15-ounce) cans hominy, rinsed and drained
    ½ cup chopped tomato
    ½ teaspoon dried basil
    ½ teaspoon salt
    ¼ teaspoon freshly ground pepper
    1 cup grated Cheddar cheese

1. Preheat oven to 350°. In a large frying pan, over medium heat, sauté sausage, breaking up into pieces, until cooked and browned. With a slotted spoon, transfer sausage onto paper towels to drain. Discard pan grease.

2. In same pan, add oil and sauté onion, celery and bell pepper until tender. Stir in cooked sausage and remaining ingredients, except cheese.

3. Pour mixture into a greased 2 1/2 quart casserole. Cover with grated cheese and bake, uncovered, for 30 to 40 minutes or until bubbly. Remove from oven and allow to set for 10 minutes before serving.

8 servings

Sweet Cheese Blintzes

Connie Walser, author of *A Collection of Blueberry Recipes*, discovered these mouth-watering blintzes in a restaurant in Moscow, Idaho. She uses blueberries from her family farm for the sauce, but other local berries will work.

BLUEBERRY SAUCE (recipe follows)
Crepes
    2 cups milk
    2 eggs
    ½ teaspoon vanilla extract
    1½ cups flour
    1 tablespoon sugar
    ½ teaspoon baking powder
    ½ teaspoon salt
    2 tablespoons butter, melted
2 tablespoons butter, for frying
Filling
    1½ cups ricotta cheese
    1 (8-ounce) package cream cheese, room temperature
    2 tablespoons sugar
    1 teaspoon cinnamon
    1 tablespoon butter, room temperature
2 tablespoons butter, for frying

1. Prepare Blueberry Sauce and set aside.

2. Make batter: Pour milk, eggs and vanilla into a blender and mix well. Sift together flour, sugar, baking powder and salt. Slowly add dry ingredients to milk mixture and blend until smooth. Add 2 tablespoons melted butter and blend again.

3. In a crepe pan, over medium, melt remaining 2 tablespoons butter. When butter is sizzling, wipe out pan lightly with paper towel. Pour about 2 tablespoons of batter in pan, swirl batter until bottom of pan is covered. Crepes should be very thin. When batter is set, turn and cook other side. With a spatula, remove and set aside. Repeat until all batter is used.

4. Make filling: In a mixing bowl, combine remaining ingredients and blend until smooth.

5. Make blintzes: Place 1 to 2 tablespoons filling on each crepe, fold in each end and roll gently. Repeat until all crepes are used.

6. In a large frying pan, over medium, melt 2 additional tablespoons butter. Fry blintzes until golden brown on both sides. Serve with warm Blueberry Sauce.   6 servings

BLUEBERRY SAUCE

½ cup water
½ cup sugar
1 tablespoon cornstarch
1 teaspoon lemon juice
2 cups blueberries

1. Combine all ingredients in a saucepan. With a whisk, stir until all lumps are gone.

2. Place pan over medium heat and continue stirring until sauce thickens, about 5 minutes.   2 cups

Breakfast Cornmeal Yeast Waffles

Guests at Kangaroo House Bed & Breakfast on Orcas Island breakfast on these delicious and unusual waffles. Most of their preparation is done the night before, so the yeast has time to work its magic overnight. The cornmeal gives a pleasing, crisp texture not found in waffles made with just wheat flour.

> 2 cups milk
> 1 package (2¼ teaspoons) active dry yeast
> ½ cup warm water
> ⅓ cup melted butter
> 1 teaspoon salt
> 1 tablespoon sugar
> 2 cups all-purpose flour
> 1 cup yellow cornmeal
> 2 large eggs, slightly beaten
> ½ teaspoon baking soda

1. In a medium saucepan, scald milk. Remove from heat and cool to luke-warm (105 to 115 degrees).

2. In a large mixing bowl, dissolve yeast in warm water. Add scalded milk, butter, salt, sugar, flour and cornmeal. Mix until batter is smooth. Cover and let stand at room temperature overnight. (Be sure to use a large bowl because the yeast mixture may double, depending on kitchen temperature.)

3. In the morning, preheat waffle iron. Stir eggs and baking soda into the yeast batter. If needed, lightly brush waffle iron surfaces with vegetable oil. Use about 1/3 cup of batter for each waffle. Cook until waffle is lightly browned. Repeat procedure for each waffle.

4. Place waffles on heated individual plates and serve with warm syrup or fresh fruit.

6-8 waffles

Mother Bird's Wonder Grain Pancakes

Islander Dorothy Bird is known for her many talents. We were delighted she agreed to share this recipe with us. The Pancake Mix can be doubled and stored in the refrigerator for future use.

PANCAKE MIX (recipe follows)
2 eggs
1 to 1½ cups milk
2 tablespoons pure maple syrup (or sugar)
1 tablespoon vegetable oil
2 tablespoons butter

1. Prepare Pancake Mix, according to directions below.

2. In a small bowl, beat eggs and stir in 1 cup milk, syrup or sugar and oil. Stir in 1 to 1 1/2 cups Pancake Mix and blend. (Do not overmix or pancakes will be tough.) Add additional milk to thin, as necessary.

3. Heat griddle or large frying pan, over medium-high heat; butter lightly. Drop the batter by heaping tablespoons and cook until bubbles formed on the pancake tops begin to burst and the bottoms are golden. Turn and cook 1 minute more. Repeat procedure with remaining batter.

4-6 servings

PANCAKE MIX

1½ cups whole wheat flour
½ cup unbleached white flour
½ cup 8-grain cereal*
¼ cup chopped almonds
1 tablespoon baking powder
¼ teaspoon baking soda
½ teaspoon salt

1. In a large bowl, combine dry ingredients and set aside. Store unused portion in an airtight container in the refrigerator.   2 3/4 cups

Available at health food stores.

Apple Oat Cereal

We loved this cold oat cereal at Windsong Bed and Breakfast, on Orcas Island. The secret is the cider!

¾ cup high-quality rolled oats
⅔ cup Martinelli apple cider
¼ cup dark brown sugar
¼ cup freshly squeezed lemon juice
¼ cup heavy cream
2 medium Granny Smith apples, unpeeled and grated
Berries, garnish

1. In a medium bowl, soak oats in cider overnight (at least eight hours).

2. In a large bowl, dissolve brown sugar in lemon juice; add oats and cider mixture. Stir in cream and apple.

3. Serve in individual bowls and garnish with berries.   4-1/2 cup servings

Rhubarb-Strawberry Sauce

The Kangaroo House, a bed and breakfast on Orcas Island, provided us with this quick and easy sauce for pancakes, pound cake, or ice cream. Use other seasonal fruits when making this simple sauce.

2 cups chopped fresh rhubarb
½ cup chopped fresh strawberries
¼-½ cup sugar

Combine rhubard and strawberries in a microwave-proof dish. Stir in sugar and toss to coat. Cover and cook on high for approximately 5 minutes, or until rhubarb is tender. Serve at desired temperature.   2 cups

Watermelon Strawberry Sorbet

Sam and Kim Haines, of Windsong Bed and Breakfast on Orcas Island, are gracious hosts. We enjoyed a remarkable meal, a lovely room and delightful company. Sam treats guests with this refreshing sorbet served as part of his delicious breakfast offerings.

¾ cup water
¾ cup sugar
2 cups seeded and pureed watermelon
1½ cups pureed strawberries
¼ cup freshly squeezed lemon juice
2 tablespoons creme de cassis
 (optional)
4-6 berries, garnish

1. Make a simple syrup: In a medium saucepan, over medium-low, combine water and sugar. Cook just until sugar dissolves, remove from heat and allow to cool to room temperature. Cover and refrigerate for at least 2 hours.

2. In an ice-cream maker, combine chilled syrup and remaining ingredients. Freeze until slushy, according to manufacturer's directions.

3. Serve in individual, chilled sorbet glasses and top each serving with a single berry.   4-6 servings

Fresh Fruit Coffee Cake

Carol Tilghman is the head baker at Georgia Johnson's Fine Catering in La Conner. She offers this mouth-watering coffee cake with a variety of fruit fillings, depending on the season.

> 1 cup unsalted butter
> 1½ cups granulated sugar
> 4 large eggs, room temperature
> 1 teaspoon vanilla extract
> 1 teaspoon almond extract
> 1½ teaspoons baking powder
> 3 cups flour
> FRUIT FILLINGS (recipes follow)
> COFFEE CAKE GLAZE (recipe follows)
> ⅓ cup toasted slivered almonds

1. Preheat oven to 350°. In a large mixing bowl, cream butter and sugar on medium speed until light in color. Add eggs, one at a time, mixing briefly after each addition. Mix in vanilla and almond extract.

2. In a medium bowl, combine baking powder and flour; beat into butter mixture. Set aside.

3. Prepare a Fruit Filling and set aside.

4. Grease and flour a 9 x 13-inch pan and with floured fingers press two-thirds of batter into the pan. Spread fruit filling over batter. With a large spoon place dollops of remaining batter on top. (The batter will not cover the fruit entirely; that is part of the eye-appeal of this cake.)

5. Place pan in the center of the oven. Bake the cake for 35 to 40 minutes or until a toothpick inserted near center comes out clean. Remove from oven and place pan on wire rack. Allow to cool for about 15 minutes before glazing. Sprinkle with toasted almonds. Serve warm or cold.

9 x 13-inch cake

STRAWBERRY FILLING

    2 cups sliced fresh strawberries
    ½ cup sugar
    2 tablespoons flour
    2 tablespoons quick-cooking tapioca

BLACKBERRY FILLING

    2 cups blackberries
    1 cup sugar
    2 tablespoons flour
    2 tablespoons quick-cooking tapioca

CHERRY FILLING

    2 cups tart pie cherries
    1 cup sugar
    ¼ cup tapioca

1. Choose appropriate filling recipe.

2. In a medium bowl, mix filling ingredients together. Allow to sit for 5 minutes before spreading over the bottom layer of coffee cake batter.

COFFEE CAKE GLAZE

    ½ cup powdered sugar
    3 tablespoons milk or light cream
    ¼ teaspoon vanilla extract

In a medium bowl, combine sugar, milk and vanilla; spread over cake with a knife.

Sour Cream Coffee Cake

Jan and Mike Russillo were innkeepers at the Kangaroo House on Orcas Island for years. This coffee cake was one of their most requested recipes.

2 cups all-purpose flour
1 cup whole wheat flour
1 tablespoon baking powder
1 teaspoon baking soda
½ teaspoon salt
1 cup butter, softened
1½ cups granulated sugar
1½ cups sour cream
1 tablespoon vanilla extract
3 eggs
Filling
    1½ cups chopped pecans
    ¾ cup packed brown sugar
    1 tablespoon ground cinnamon

1. Preheat oven to 350°. Grease and lightly flour a 9 x 13-inch pan or a 10-inch Bundt pan. In a medium bowl, sift together flours, baking powder, baking soda and salt. Set aside.

2. In a large mixing bowl, cream butter and sugar. Add sour cream and vanilla and mix thoroughly. Beat in eggs, one at a time; mix well after each addition.

3. Slowly add reserved flour to cream mixture, mix just until smooth. Spoon 2/3 of the batter into the prepared pan.

4. Prepare filling: In a small bowl, combine pecans, brown sugar and cinnamon. Sprinkle the filling evenly over the batter. Distribute remaining batter evenly over the filling. (Don't worry if it doesn't completely cover.)

5. Place pan in oven and bake for 40-45 minutes or until toothpick inserted in center of cake comes out clean. Remove from oven and cool on a rack for 5 minutes. Serve while warm.   12 servings

Marionberry Muffins

La Vie en Rose Bakery in Anacortes offers these delectable berry-filled muffins as a great way to greet the morning.

4½ cups all-purpose flour
2¼ cups sugar
1½ tablespoons baking powder
1¼ teaspoons salt
1 cup vegetable oil
5 eggs
2½ cups milk
1 tablespoon vanilla extract
4 cups marionberries
Streusel Topping
    ¾ cup all-purpose flour
    1¼ cups oats
    ¾ cup brown sugar
    6 tablespoons vegetable oil

1. Preheat oven to 350°. Grease top of large-size muffin tin and line with paper cups.

2. In a large bowl, sift together dry ingredients (flour through salt) and set aside.

3. In a mixing bowl, combine oil, eggs, milk and vanilla and beat until well blended. Add to dry ingredients and stir until combined. Do not overmix or the muffins will be tough and chewy.

4. Fold marionberries into batter. Spoon batter into prepared muffin tin.

5. In a small bowl, combine streusel ingredients and sprinkle equal amounts over the muffin tops.

6. Bake muffins for 40-50 minutes or until a toothpick inserted in the center of the muffins comes out clean. Remove the muffins from oven and cool on a wire rack.

12 large muffins

Paskhal'niy Kulich

This Easter bread from Olga Gorman provides the smell and taste of the traditional Russian Orthodox Easter celebration. We were delighted she shared this old family recipe with us. Although time-consuming, it is well worth the trouble.

> 2 cups milk
> 1 ½ tablespoons yeast
> 7 cups unbleached white flour
> 1 cup butter
> 7 egg yolks
> 1½ cups granulated sugar
> 1 teaspoon salt
> 1 tablespoon cognac
> 1 tablespoon vanilla
> ¾ cup raisins, if desired
> ¾ cup sliced almonds, if desired
> ½ cup candied orange peel, if desired
> Glaze
> > ¾ cup sugar
> > 1 tablespoon honey
> > ½ teaspoon powdered ginger
> > ½ teaspoon allspice
> > ⅓ cup finely minced nuts
> > ¼ cup minced raisins
> > ¼ cup water

1. Make sponge: In a medium saucepan, heat milk over medium until it is lukewarm (not hot!). Put yeast in a large mixing bowl; pour milk over yeast and allow mixture to proof 10-15 minutes. Add 3 1/2 cups of flour and mix thoroughly. Cover bowl with a towel and allow to rise in a warm place about 1 to 2 hours. The sponge is done when dough more than doubles and then begins to sag.

2. In a small saucepan, melt butter over medium; remove from heat and allow to cool. In a large mixing bowl, beat egg yolks with the sugar until pale. Add egg mixture, remaining 3 1/2 cups flour, melted butter, salt, cognac and vanilla into sponge. Add raisins, almonds and orange peel, as desired. Mix to blend.

3. On a lightly floured board, knead the dough for 7 to 10 minutes. Put dough in clean, large bowl, cover with towel and allow it to rise in a warm place. Let it rise twice; punch down each time. Let dough rise for the third time and place it on a floured surface.

4. Shape dough into 6 loaves. Butter and lightly flour 6 small loaf pans. Place dough into pans; dough should fill one-third of the pan. (Do not use loaf pans that are too large.) Let dough rise in a warm place until it reaches the top of bread pan (about an hour.)

5. Preheat oven to 400°. Bake loaves for 15 minutes at 400°; reduce heat to 375° and continue baking for 45 minutes more. Remove from oven, turn loaves out of pans and allow to cool on wire racks before glazing.

6. Prepare glaze: In a small saucepan, combine all glaze ingredients and bring to a boil over medium-high heat. Boil for 10 minutes. Cool for 10 to 15 minutes, glaze is thick but spreadable. Brush loaves with glaze.

6 loaves

Challah French Toast

Kangaroo House, on Orcas Island, is a small country inn. Be sure to ask the innkeepers how it acquired this unusual name. It is a fine example of a traditional bed and breakfast providing the spirit of warmth, hospitality and good cheer. This decadent and deliciously rich toast gets rave reviews from their guests. The crispy crust of cornflake crumbs adds a pleasing texture.

6 eggs, slightly beaten
2 cups light cream
¼ cup rum
1 tablespoon orange zest
1 cup sugar
½ teaspoon cinnamon
½ teaspoon nutmeg
3 cups cornflake crumbs
1 loaf Challah Bread, sliced ½-inch thick
Butter

1. In a large bowl, whisk together first 7 ingredients (eggs through nutmeg). Pour mixture into a shallow bowl. Place cornflake crumbs in a separate shallow bowl.

2. Dip bread slices into egg mixture, then in cornflake crumbs to coat. Place on a baking sheet and let sit for 10 to 15 minutes before cooking.

3. In a large frying pan, over medium-high heat, melt 1 tablespoon butter and fry bread slices until crispy and golden brown. Do not crowd pan. Repeat procedure with remaining bread. Add additional butter, as needed for frying.

4. Place toast on heated individual plates and dust with powdered sugar. Serve with syrup or fresh fruit.

8 servings

Raspberry Scones

The charming Orcas Hotel has been receiving guests since 1904. Visitors can enjoy these fruit-laced scones while sitting in the cozy bakery or out on the deck observing the comings and goings of boats in the harbor below. Other berries or dried fruits can be substituted for the raspberries.

    4 cups unbleached all-purpose flour
    ⅔ cup sugar
    1 tablespoon baking powder
    1 teaspoon baking soda
    ½ teaspoon salt
    ¾ cup cold butter, cut into small pieces
    1 cup buttermilk
    2 eggs, slightly beaten
    1 tablespoon vanilla extract
    3 tablespoons orange or lemon zest
    1½ cups raspberries (or ⅔ cup raisins)
    1 egg yolk
    1 tablespoon water
    1 tablespoon coarse raw sugar

1. Preheat oven to 375°. In a large mixing bowl, combine flour, sugar, baking powder, soda and salt. Mix in butter until the mixture resembles coarse meal.

2. Make a well in the center of the flour mixture and pour in buttermilk, eggs and vanilla. Stir batter with a fork until dough holds together. (Be careful not to overwork.) Gently fold in zest and raspberries or raisins.

3. On a lightly floured board, knead dough for 5 to 6 turns. Divide dough in half and form two 7-inch rounds about 1 inch high. Place on an ungreased baking sheet and with a knife score each round into quarters. In a small bowl, make an egg wash by mixing egg yolk and 1 tablespoon water. Brush wash on dough circles and sprinkle with raw sugar.

4. Bake for about 30 minutes, or until a toothpick inserted in the center of the scones comes out clean. The scones should be golden brown. Serve warm with butter.   8 scones

Rosemary Focaccia

Focaccia is a rustic Italian flatbread that can be seasoned with a variety of toppings: olive oil, slivers of garlic, sautéed onions, olives or Parmesan cheese. Enjoy it as is, or use it to make Italian sandwiches (panini) by splitting the focaccia horizontally and filling it with a tasty stuffing, such as: fresh mozzarella with tomato and basil; grilled eggplant and grilled red pepper; or sliced pork tenderloin, accented with 1/3 part Dijon mustard and 2/3 parts apricot jam.

> 1 package active dried yeast (2 ½ teaspoons)
> 1 cup warm water
> 2 tablespoons extra-virgin olive oil
> 1 teaspoon salt
> 2½ to 3 cups unbleached white flour
> 1 scant tablespoon cornmeal
> 1 tablespoon extra-virgin olive oil
> 1 tablespoon fresh rosemary leaves
> 1 teaspoon coarsely ground sea salt

1. In a large bowl, dissolve yeast in warm water. Allow to proof for 3 minutes; stir in oil and salt. Add flour, 1 cup at a time, and mix until dough begins to ball and pull away from side of bowl.

2. Knead on a lightly floured board until dough is smooth and elastic. Place dough in greased bowl, turn over to grease top. Cover with plastic wrap. Let rise in warm (80°) place until dough doubles, about 1 hour.

3. Punch down the dough and roll it into a 10-inch round about 1/2-inch-thick. Place dough onto a generously oiled heavy-duty baking sheet. Sprinkle with cornmeal.

4. Drizzle with 1 tablespoon olive oil. Garnish with rosemary leaves, pressing them into the dough with your fingers. Sprinkle with salt. Let the dough rise for 20 minutes.

5. Preheat oven to 450°. Bake focaccia in lower third of the oven for 20 minutes or until golden brown. Remove from oven, cut into wedge-shaped pieces and serve warm.   1 focaccia

Jalapeno Beer Cornbread

The Front Street Cafe in Friday Harbor serves this savory bread with their Black Bean Chili.

1½ cups unbleached white flour
2 cups cornmeal
½ cup sugar
1½ tablespoons baking powder
1 teaspoon salt
2 cups corn kernels, fresh or thawed
⅓ cup sliced jalapeno chili peppers, reserving 2 slices
½ cup light cream
1 (12-ounce) can or bottle beer
1-2 tablespoons melted butter

1. Preheat oven to 375°. Combine dry ingredients in a large bowl and mix thoroughly. Blend in remaining ingredients, except melted butter. Do not overmix.

2. Grease a loaf pan and pour batter into pan. Top with jalapeno slices and drizzle with melted butter.

3. Bake for 50-60 minutes or until a toothpick inserted in the center of the loaf comes out clean. Remove pan from oven and place pan on a wire rack. Slice loaf and serve warm.   1 loaf

Parmesan Pita Triangles

These crispy toasts are easy to make. Serve with our Hummus as an appetizer or as an accompaniment to a salad, soup or entree.

3 pita breads
¼ cup butter or margarine
1 clove garlic, minced
1 tablespoon minced fresh parsley
2 tablespoons freshly grated Parmesan cheese
⅛ teaspoon paprika

1. Preheat oven to 350°. With a knife, cut outside rim of each pita bread to separate into two halves. Set aside.

2. In a small saucepan, melt butter over medium heat. Stir in garlic and parsley. Brush butter mixture lightly over pita halves. Sprinkle with cheese and paprika.

3. Cut pita halves into quarters using a knife or kitchen scissors. Arrange in a single layer on an ungreased baking sheet. Bake until golden brown, about 12 minutes. Serve warm. 6 servings

Desserts

VINCE STREANO

Washington State Ferry in the San Juan Islands

Claudia's North Beach Chocolate Cake

This rich, moist sheet cake is perfect for a crowd. We have served it for years at family picnics and it always gets rave reviews.

1 cup butter or margarine
1 cup water
¼ cup unsweetened cocoa
2 cups unbleached white flour
2 cups sugar
2 eggs, beaten
1 teaspoon soda
½ teaspoon salt
½ cup sour cream
CHOCOLATE ICING (recipe follows)

1. Preheat oven to 350°. In a medium saucepan, combine butter, water and cocoa. Bring to a boil and remove from heat. While mixture is hot, add remaining cake ingredients and stir until smooth.

2. Grease and flour a 12 x 18-inch sheet pan. Pour batter into pan and bake for 30 minutes or until a toothpick inserted in the center of cake comes out clean. Remove pan from oven and place on a wire rack.

3. Prepare Chocolate Icing and spread on warm cake.   24 servings

CHOCOLATE ICING

½ cup butter or margarine
¼ cup and 2 tablespoons milk
¼ cup unsweetened cocoa
1 teaspoon vanilla
1 (16-ounce) box powdered sugar (4 cups)
1 cup coarsely chopped nuts

1. In a saucepan, over medium-high, stir to combine butter, milk and cocoa. Bring to a boil and remove from heat.

2. Add remaining ingredients and stir until smooth. Stir in additional milk if icing is too stiff.

Cleo's Chocolate Mocha Cake

If you are passionate about chocolate, you will love this moist cake enhanced with a creamy, rich chocolate frosting. It is the most requested cake at our birthday celebrations.

    1 cup semi-sweet chocolate chips
    ¼ cup prepared coffee
    2 cups sifted cake flour
    1 teaspoon baking soda
    ¼ teaspoon salt
    ¾ cup butter or margarine
    1¾ cups sugar
    3 eggs
    1 teaspoon vanilla extract
    1 cup buttermilk
    CHOCOLATE CREAM FROSTING (recipe follows)

1. Preheat oven to 375°. Grease and flour two 9-inch round cake pans or one 9 x 13-inch pan; set aside.

2. Place chocolate and coffee in a small heavy saucepan, over low; heat until chocolate is melted. Set aside to cool.

3. Sift together cake flour, baking soda and salt. Set aside.

4. In a large mixing bowl, cream together butter and sugar. Add eggs, one at a time, beating after each addition. Blend in vanilla, melted chocolate and coffee.

5. With beater at low speed, alternating between the two, add the dry ingredients and buttermilk to the chocolate mixture in three steps, ending with flour. Beat well after each addition.

6. Pour batter into prepared pans and bake until a toothpick inserted in the center of cake comes out clean. Allow about 25 minutes for round pans or 35 minutes for a 9 x 13-inch pan.

7. Remove cake from oven and set on wire rack. If using layer pans, let sit for 5 minutes then invert the pans over wire racks to release the cake. Let the cake cool completely before frosting.

8. Spread cake with frosting. Serve with ice cream. If using our Chocolate Cream Frosting, cake must be refrigerated. 10-12 servings

CHOCOLATE CREAM FROSTING

Use this recipe with the 9 x 13-inch cake. Double the recipe if making the layered cake.

    1 cup semi-sweet chocolate chips
    1 cup heavy cream
    1 (3-ounce) package cream cheese, room temperature
    2 tablespoons butter or margarine
    1 teaspoon vanilla extract
    1 cup powdered sugar

1. Place chocolate in a small heavy saucepan, over low; heat until chocolate is melted. Set aside to cool.

2. In a large mixing bowl, beat heavy cream until stiff. Transfer whipped cream to another bowl; set aside.

3. In the same large mixing bowl, beat together cream cheese and butter until smooth. Mix in cooled chocolate and vanilla. Gradually add sugar and beat well. Fold in reserved whipped cream.

Mocha Cheesecake

"As moist and creamy as imaginable, this cake balances chocolate and coffee flavors perfectly," writes Carol Foster in her cookbook, *Cooking with Coffee*. We found her description deliciously accurate. The cake will keep for a week if refrigerated.

Crust
>   1½ cups graham cracker crumbs
>   1/4 cup sugar
>   6 tablespoons unsalted butter, softened

Filling
>   8 ounces semi-sweet chocolate, grated
>   3 tablespoons heavy cream
>   1½ pounds cream cheese, softened
>   1 cup sugar
>   3 eggs
>   1½ cups sour cream
>   ½ cup brewed espresso or double-strength dark roast coffee, cooled slightly
>   2 teaspoons vanilla extract

Chocolate curls*, garnish

1. Make crust: In a medium bowl, blend the graham cracker crumbs with the sugar and butter. Press evenly onto the bottom of a 9-inch springform pan and chill if made ahead. Preheat oven to 350°.

2. Prepare filling: In a heavy small saucepan, over low heat, melt the chocolate and cream, stirring constantly. Set aside to cool slightly.

3. In a mixing bowl or a food processor, beat the cream cheese with the sugar until light and smooth. Beat in the eggs, one at a time. Blend in the melted chocolate, sour cream, espresso and vanilla; beat until smooth.

4. Pour the mixture into the springform pan. Bake in the center of the oven for 60 to 70 minutes. (The center of the cake will jiggle, but it will solidify while cooling.)

5. Remove the cake from the oven and cool on a wire rack. Chill thoroughly.

6. Remove the springform pan ring and garnish the cheesecake with shaved chocolate curls. To serve, slice cake into wedges with a knife dipped in hot water.

9-inch cake

*To make chocolate curls, melt 2 ounces semi-sweet chocolate and pour onto a hard, flat surface. When the chocolate has set, hold a sharp knife at a 45-degree angle and push it along the chocolate to form curls. Repeat until all the chocolate is used.

White Chocolate Ice Cream With Blackberry Sauce In Hazelnut Cookie Cups

Chef Gretchen Allison of Duck Soup Inn on San Juan Island makes this wonderful dessert when wild island blackberries are at their peak. It's typical of the fare at her charming country restaurant nestled in an old-growth forest–the perfect setting for a romantic evening of fine dining.

> 1 cup whole milk
> 3 cups cream
> ½ cup granulated sugar
> 1 teaspoon vanilla extract
> ⅛ teaspoon salt
> 8 ounces Belgium white chocolate, broken into chunks
> HAZELNUT TUILE COOKIE CUPS (recipe follows)
> BLACKBERRY SAUCE (recipe follows)
> Powdered sugar, garnish

1. Prepare ice cream: In the top of a double boiler, combine milk, cream, sugar, vanilla and salt. When sugar is dissolved, add white chocolate. Scrape sides and stir every few minutes; whisk to dissolve any lumps. Remove from heat and cool to room temperature.

2. Pour chocolate mixture into ice cream maker and follow manufacturer's directions for ice cream. Cover and store in freezer.

3. Prepare Hazelnut Tuile Cookie Cups according to directions.

4. Prepare Blackberry Sauce according to directions.

5. When ready to serve, spoon the ice cream into cookie cups and drizzle with Blackberry Sauce. Serve on individual plates; dust with powdered sugar.   8 servings

HAZELNUT TUILE COOKIE CUPS

7 tablespoons butter, softened
1 cup granulated sugar
4 large egg whites
½ cup plus 2 tablespoons all-purpose flour
⅔ cup finely ground hazelnuts
1 teaspoon vanilla

1. Preheat oven to 300°. In a large mixing bowl, whip butter and sugar together. Beat egg whites into sugar mixture; add flour and mix. Stir in hazelnuts and vanilla.

2. Line cookie sheets with parchment paper. For each cookie, use 3 to 4 tablespoons dough. Using a spatula, spread dough out to a 5-inch diameter circle. (Each cookie sheet will only hold 2 to 3 cookies.)

3. Bake cookies for 10 minutes, or until they begin to brown. Remove from oven; allow to sit for a few minutes. Drape each cookie over the bottom of a drinking glass to form a cup. (If the cookies crisp too much to mold, heat them in the oven to soften.)

4. If made ahead, store cookie cups in covered container.   8 cookies

BLACKBERRY SAUCE

2 cups blackberries, fresh or frozen
1 tablespoon Triple Sec liqueur
⅓ cup sugar

1. In a small saucepan, over medium-high, combine all ingredients. Stir to break down berries. Cook as little as possible.

2. To remove seeds, strain sauce through a sieve into a bowl. Set aside to cool, cover and refrigerate.   2 cups

Italian Plum Tart

Italian plums are plentiful on the islands in August and September. Several years ago, a box of freshly picked plums was delivered to our door by Guemes Islanders Anne and Phil McCracken, accompanied by this easy and delicious recipe.

2 cups unbleached white flour
2 tablespoons sugar
1 teaspoon baking powder
¼ teaspoon salt
¾ cups chilled butter, cut into small pieces
1 egg, beaten
2 tablespoons cold water
1½ pounds Italian plums, washed
½ cup sugar (less if plums are sweet)
¼ cup sugar
2 tablespoons flour
1 teaspoon cinnamon
¼ cup slivered almonds
2 tablespoons butter
Whipped cream

1. In a medium bowl, combine flour, sugar, baking powder and salt. With a pastry blender or fork, cut in butter until mixture resembles coarse meal. Add egg and water until evenly moist. Form into a ball and transfer to a 10-inch pie pan. With fingers, press dough into bottom and sides of pan.

2. Preheat oven to 375°. Cut plums in half, discard pits. Place fruit flesh-side down on dough, in a circular pattern, overlapping slightly. Sprinkle evenly with 1/2 cup sugar.

4. In a small bowl, combine remaining 1/4 cup sugar, flour, cinnamon and almonds. Sprinkle over plums. Dot with additional butter.

5. Bake for 40-50 minutes. Plums should juice and bubble. Cut into wedges and serve with whipped cream, if desired. 8 servings

Mormor's Chocolate Roll (Chokladrulltarta)

This Scandinavian specialty was passed down to Ingrid Kassler from her mother Elinor Stahlbrand. It is a favorite family dessert for birthdays and other special occasions. For a variation, fill the roll with our Chocolate Ganache.

3 eggs
¾ cup sugar
⅓ cup potato flour
2 teaspoons baking powder
2 tablespoons unsweetened cocoa
Filling
    ½ cup butter, room temperature
    ½ cup powdered sugar
    2 egg yolks
    1 teaspoon vanilla extract

1. Prepare cake: Preheat oven to 425°. In a large mixing bowl, beat eggs and sugar until well blended. Sift flour, baking powder and cocoa into a bowl and add to egg mixture. Mix to blend.

2. Line a 10 x 14-inch jellyroll pan with parchment paper and pour batter into pan. Bake for 5 to 8 minutes.

3. Remove cake from oven and turn onto a tea towel sprinkled with powdered sugar. Remove paper from cake and place the jellyroll pan over the cake. Leave covered until cool, about 20 minutes.

4. Prepare filling: In a large bowl, combine butter and sugar. Beat until mixture is smooth and fluffy. Add egg yolks and vanilla; mix well.

5. Spread filling over cooled cake and roll cake lengthwise. Wrap in foil or waxed paper and refrigerate overnight.

6. Cut into slices to serve.

1 cake roll

CHOCOLATE GANACHE

10 ounces semisweet chocolate
2/3 cup heavy cream
1 tablespoon honey

1. Using a large knife, cut chocolate into 1/2-inch pieces. Place into the bowl of a food processor and process until finely chopped; set aside.

2. In a small saucepan, bring cream and honey to a boil. Slowly pour hot cream mixture over chocolate with processor running.

3. Place ganache in a bowl, cover and refrigerate until needed.

1 1/2 cups

Pineapple Apricot Cake

Rosario Resort is gaining respect for consistently offering excellent cuisine in their elegant restaurant located in the Moran mansion. Pastry Chef David Schultze trained at the Cordon Bleu in England. His talent has brought a new dimension to the restaurant's offerings. This luscious two-layer cake with an orange and apricot frosting is one example of his expertise.

1 cup diced canned pineapple, reserving juice
½ cup pineapple juice
½ cup diced dried apricots
½ cup golden raisins
½ cup toasted coconut
1½ cups grated carrots
½ cup chopped toasted pecans
3 cups all-purpose flour
2 teaspoons baking powder
1 teaspoon ground cinnamon
½ teaspoon salt
1 cup unsalted butter
2 cups granulated sugar
3 eggs
ORANGE APRICOT FROSTING (recipe follows)

1. Preheat oven to 325°. Grease 2 (10-inch) round cake pans, line with parch-

ment and grease again. In a large bowl, combine first 7 ingredients (pineapple through pecans) and set aside.

2. Sift dry ingredients together into a large bowl and set aside.

3. In a large mixing bowl, cream butter and sugar together. Add eggs, beating them in one at a time. Fold in dry ingredients and fruit mixture. Pour batter into prepared pans.

4. Place on rack in center of oven and bake about 45 to 50 minutes or until a toothpick inserted in the center of the cakes comes out clean. Remove pans from oven and place on wire racks to cool for about 10 minutes.

5. Invert cakes over wire racks to release the cakes. Cool completely before frosting.

6. Prepare Orange Apricot Frosting while cake layers cool. Place one layer on cake plate. Spread the top with frosting and place other layer on top. Finish by frosting sides and top of cake.　　　　　1 10-inch layer cake

ORANGE APRICOT FROSTING

12 ounces cream cheese
2 tablespoons orange liqueur
½ teaspoon vanilla extract
¼ cup powdered sugar, sifted
¼ cup chopped toasted pecans
¼ cup diced dried apricots
¼ cup toasted coconut

1. In a mixing bowl, beat cream cheese until fluffy. On low speed, add liqueur, vanilla and sugar; blend until smooth.

2. Fold in pecans, apricots and coconut. Spread frosting on cake, as directed.

2 cups

Apricot Almond Tart

Be sure to save room for dessert while dining at Bella Isola Ristorante in Anacortes. Baker and Pastry Chef Kathy Longstreet creates luscious sweet treats as well as rustic loaves of Italian bread and foccacia.

Crust
   ¾ cup almonds
   ¾ cup plus 1½ tablespoons sugar
   10 tablespoons unsalted butter
   1 large egg
   1½ teaspoons rum
   1¾ cups all-purpose flour
   ¼ teaspoon cinnamon
   Pinch salt
Frangipane
   ½ cup unsalted butter
   ½ cup sugar
   8 ounces almond paste
   ½ teaspoon almond extract
   1 large egg
   ½ cup plus 1 tablespoon all-purpose flour
Filling
   1½ (15½-ounce) cans drained apricot halves
   1 (8-ounce) jar apricot preserves
   zest of 1 lemon
Garnish
   ¼ cup thinly sliced raw almonds

1. Prepare crust: Preheat oven to 350°. In a shallow pan toast almonds about 5 minutes or until light brown. Remove from oven and set aside to cool. Place nuts in a food processor and pulse until finely ground; set aside.

2. Increase oven temperature to 375°. In a large mixing bowl, beat sugar and butter until light and fluffy. Add egg, ground almonds and rum; continue to beat until well mixed.

3. Sift together flour, cinnamon and salt; add to butter mixture and mix until combined.

4. Press a thin layer of crust mixture (1/8-inch) onto bottom and sides of tart

pan. (It helps to work with wet fingers.) Reserve remaining crust mixture for decoration on top of tart. Cover crust with plastic wrap and place in freezer until firm.

5. Prepare Frangipane: In a large mixing bowl, beat butter, sugar and almond paste until light and fluffy. Gradually add almond extract and egg. Add flour and mix until thoroughly combined.

6. Remove tart shell from freezer and spread a layer of Frangipane over crust, 1/4-inch thick. (If you have additional Frangipane reserve for tea cookies.)

7. Place tart pan on a cookie sheet and bake until it puffs up and barely begins to brown, about 5 to 10 minutes. Remove from oven and set aside to cool.

8. Prepare filling: In a large bowl, combine apricot halves, preserves and lemon zest. Pour into tart shell and arrange apricots domed side up evenly over surface. Sprinkle almonds over top.

9. Preheat oven to 350°. Put reserved crust mixture in pastry bag and pipe 1-inch rosettes around outer edge of tart. (They should touch one another.)

10. Bake until rosettes are light brown and jam mixture begins to bubble slightly, about 20-30 minutes. Remove from oven and cool. Serve at room temperature.   1 tart

To make mouth-watering tea cookies: Preheat oven to 350°. Combine leftover crust dough and Frangipane; place in a pastry bag. Make rosettes on a cookie sheet and bake until lightly browned, about 10 minutes.

Lemon Tart

Laura and Bill Thomas are the owners of La Vie en Rose, a French bakery in Anacortes. We encourage you to stop in at this popular gathering place and try their wonderful breads, desserts and delicatessen items.

Pastry Shell
- 1½ cups unbleached white flour
- ¼ cup sugar
- ¼ teaspoon salt
- ½ cup butter, chilled
- 1 egg
- 1 to 3 tablespoons ice water

LEMON TART FILLING (recipe follows)
- 2 tablespoons powdered sugar

1. In a large bowl, combine flour, sugar and salt. With a pastry blender or fork, cut in butter until mixture resembles coarse meal.

2. In a small bowl, beat egg slightly. Add egg to flour mixture and mix until evenly moistened.

3. Add ice water, 1 tablespoon at a time. Mix with a fork until dough just holds together. (Be careful not to overwork.)

4. On a lightly floured board, roll dough out to 1/4-inch thickness. Transfer dough to an ungreased 11-inch tart pan and press evenly into all grooves. Trim away any excess dough. Cover and refrigerate for at least an hour.

5. Preheat oven to 350°. Prepare Lemon Tart Filling.

6. Pour filling into chilled shell and place in center of oven. Bake 20 to 25 minutes or until filling is set. Tart should be evenly golden. Remove from oven and cool on wire rack. Dust with powdered sugar. Serve warm or cold.

11-inch tart

LEMON TART FILLING

½ cup butter, room temperature
1 cup sugar
3 eggs
¼ cup fresh lemon juice
1 teaspoon lemon extract

1. In a large mixing bowl, cream butter and sugar together until fluffy.
2. Beat in eggs, one at a time, scraping bowl after each addition. Gently mix in lemon juice and extract.   1 1/2 cups

Blueberry Peach Pie

This recipe comes to us from Walser Farms located in the Skagit Valley. Enjoy this unique combination of fresh fruit.

Pastry for double-crust 9-inch pie
3 cups peeled and sliced peaches
2 cups blueberries
2 tablespoons lemon juice
1⅓ cups sugar
2 tablespoons quick-cooking tapioca
⅛ teaspoon salt
2 tablespoons butter
1 egg yolk
Ice cream (optional)

1. Preheat oven to 425°. Line pie plate with bottom crust; set aside.

2. In a large bowl, place prepared fruit and sprinkle with lemon juice; set aside. In a medium bowl, combine sugar, tapioca and salt. Pour mixture over fruit and toss gently to blend.

3. Pour fruit mixture into pie shell, dot with butter. Top with crust, flute edges and cut steam vents.

4. Brush crust with egg yolk beaten with 1 tablespoon water. Bake for 45-50 minutes or until fruit is tender and crust is golden. Serve warm with ice cream, if desired.

9-inch pie

Wild Blackberry Cobbler

It's a sure sign of summer when you discover the first ripe wild blackberries in late June. Islanders are notoriously secretive about the location of their own private patch. For exceptional flavor, make this cobbler with the small wild blackberries.

Filling
 8 cups blackberries, cleaned
 ⅓ cup flour
 1½ cups sugar
 2 tablespoons lemon juice
 1 teaspoon minced lemon zest
Biscuits
 2 cups flour
 ½ teaspoon salt
 4 teaspoons baking powder
 4 tablespoons sugar
 ½ cup butter
 ½ cup cold milk
 1 teaspoon vanilla extract
2 tablespoons butter
½ teaspoon cinnamon
1 tablespoon sugar
Vanilla ice cream

1. Prepare filling: In a large bowl, combine filling ingredients. Taste and add additional sugar, if needed. Set aside.

2. Preheat oven to 350°. Prepare biscuits: In a large mixing bowl, combine flour, salt, baking powder and sugar. With a pastry blender, cut in butter until mixture has the consistency of coarse meal. Stir in milk and vanilla. Do not overwork dough; set aside.

3. Pour blackberry mixture into a greased 9 x 13-inch baking pan. Dot berries with remaining 2 tablespoons butter. Drop the prepared biscuit dough by spoonfuls on top of the berry mixture, until almost covered. Sprinkle the cinnamon and sugar over dough. Bake for 40 minutes until fruit is bubbling and the biscuits are golden brown. Remove from oven and cool on a rack. Serve with vanilla ice cream.   10-12 servings

Raspberry Baked Alaska

This luscious dessert is a real show-stopper. Raspberry-rippled ice cream and lady fingers are hidden under clouds of snowy meringue resting in a pool of chocolate orange sauce.

CHOCOLATE ORANGE SAUCE (recipe follows)
18 lady fingers
⅓ cup orange-flavored liqueur (Grand Marnier, Triple Sec), divided
2 cups fresh raspberries or 1 (10-ounce) frozen package, thawed
3 pints vanilla ice cream, slightly thawed
4 egg whites, room temperature
⅛ teaspoon salt
⅛ teaspoon cream of tartar
⅔ cup sugar

1. Prepare Chocolate Orange Sauce following directions.

2. Line the bottom and side of a 9-inch pie plate with about 12 of the lady fingers. Allow 1/2-inch of the lady fingers to extend beyond the plate rim. Drizzle with half of the liqueur.

3. In a medium bowl, using a potato masher, crush berries. (If using fresh berries, add 1/2 cup sugar.)

4. In a large bowl, place softened ice cream. Drop spoonfuls of raspberries onto ice cream. With a knife, cut through berries and ice cream to create a marbled effect. Do not overmix.

5. Spoon half of the ice cream mixture over lady fingers. Top with remaining lady fingers and drizzle with remaining liqueur. Spoon remaining ice cream mixture over lady fingers. Cover and freeze until firm, about 4 hours or up to 2 weeks.

6. About 20 minutes before serving, preheat oven to 500°. (If Chocolate Sauce is in refrigerator, remove and heat through.)

7. Prepare meringue: In a medium bowl, at high speed, beat egg whites, salt and cream of tartar until soft peaks form. Continue beating at high speed and add sugar, 2 tablespoons at a time, until whites become stiff and glossy.

8. Remove pie from freezer and spread meringue over top, sealing to edge. With a knife, swirl meringue for an attractive finish.

9. Bake 3 to 4 minutes, until meringue is lightly browned. On individual plates, spoon 2 tablespoons of warm Chocolate Orange Sauce to the right of the center. Place a slice of pie in the center of the plate. Serve immediately.

8-10 servings

CHOCOLATE ORANGE SAUCE

This sauce can be made ahead and refrigerated. Heat before using.

8 ounces semi-sweet chocolate
1¼ cups fresh orange juice
½ cup unsalted butter
¼ cup orange-flavored liqueur (Grand Marnier, Triple Sec)

1. In a small heavy saucepan, over low heat, combine chocolate and orange juice. Stir constantly until chocolate has melted. Do not overcook.

2. Add butter and liqueur; whisk to blend. Use immediately or cover and refrigerate.

2 cups

Apple Green Chili Pie

Our island friend Mary O'Hern travels to the Southwest every year. During her stay there, she prepares several of these pies for the Donkey Dust Cafe in Tularosa, New Mexico, and they sell out before they even cool! Butter is the key ingredient in her rich crusts. Mary's Southwest apple pie is always a favorite at island gatherings.

Pastry for double-crust, 9-inch pie
1 tablespoon sugar
6 large baking apples (Granny Smith or Golden Delicious)
    (4 cups peeled, cored and sliced)
1 cup all-purpose flour
1 cup sugar
2 teaspoons cinnamon
½ to ¾ cup heavy cream
1 (5-ounce) can mild green chilies, chopped
2 tablespoons butter
2 teaspoons heavy cream
2 teaspoons sugar

1. Preheat oven to 375°. Line a pie plate with bottom crust and sprinkle with 1 tablespoon sugar; set aside.

2. In a large bowl, combine apple slices, flour, sugar and cinnamon. Pour in cream and stir to blend with extra flour to make a thick creamy consistency. (At this point, you can taste a piece of apple to see if more sugar is needed.) Stir in green chilies and mix thoroughly.

3. Pour apple filling into bottom crust and dot with butter. Cover with top crust and crimp edges. Brush top crust with cream and sprinkle with sugar. Cut vents and bake for 1 hour. Cover outer edges with foil to keep from over-browning, if necessary.   9-inch pie

Deep Dish Apple Pie

This fall dessert is sure to please any apple pie lover. The caramel filling has a rich, spicy flavor.

Filling
- 6 cups sliced tart baking apples (Gravenstein or Granny Smith)
- 1 cup sugar
- ¼ cup all-purpose flour
- 1 teaspoon cinnamon
- ¼ teaspoon nutmeg
- ¼ teaspoon ground cloves
- 1 tablespoon water
- 1 tablespoon rum or brandy
- 2 tablespoons butter or margarine

Crust
- 1½ cups all-purpose flour
- ¼ teaspoon salt
- ½ cup margarine
- 4-5 tablespoons ice water
- ½ teaspoon cinnamon
- 2 tablespoons sugar

Ice cream (optional)

1. Preheat oven to 400°. Prepare filling: In a large mixing bowl, combine all filling ingredients, except butter. Pour mixture into a buttered 9 x 13-inch baking dish and dot with butter.

2. Prepare crust: In a large mixing bowl, combine flour and salt. With a pastry blender or fork, cut in margarine until mixture resembles coarse meal. Sprinkle 1 tablespoon of ice water over flour mixture, gently mix with a fork. Add additional water until dough holds together.

3. Form dough into a ball and flatten on lightly floured surface. Roll dough about 1/8-inch thick and place on top of apple mixture, leaving a 1/2-inch overhang. Fold outside edges of dough against sides of pan and flute.

4. Cut 4 slits in crust for steam vents. Sprinkle with cinnamon and sugar. Bake for 40 minutes until filling is bubbly and crust is golden brown. Serve warm with ice cream.

8 servings

Carrot Cake
With Cream Cheese Frosting

Kathy Mohrweiss owns and operates Kathy's Pies and Cakes, a baking and catering service in Friday Harbor. This cake is always a hit with her customers.

2¼ cups all-purpose flour
2 cups sugar
2 teaspoons baking soda
2 teaspoons baking powder
2 teaspoons cinnamon
1 teaspoon salt
4 eggs
1⅓ cups corn oil
2½ cups grated carrots
1 cup pineapple chunks, chopped
¾ cups chopped walnuts
CREAM CHEESE FROSTING (recipe follows)

1. Preheat oven to 350°. Grease and lightly flour 2 (9-inch) round cake pans. In a large mixing bowl, sift dry ingredients and mix slightly. Add eggs, one at a time, beating after each addition. Pour in oil and mix again.

2. Stir grated carrots and pineapple into batter. Do not overmix.

3. Fold in walnuts and pour batter into prepared pans. Bake about 35 minutes or until a toothpick inserted in the center of the cake comes out clean. Remove pans from oven and place on wire racks to cool for about 10 minutes.

4. Invert cakes over wire racks to release the cakes. Cool completely before frosting.

5. Prepare frosting while cakes cool. Spread cakes with frosting.

9-inch layer cake

CREAM CHEESE FROSTING

1 cup butter, room temperature
6 ounces cream cheese
2 teaspoons vanilla
4 cups powdered sugar

In a large mixing bowl, combine butter and cream cheese. Beat until mixture is smooth and fluffy. Add vanilla and powdered sugar and mix well. Turn mixer to high speed and whip for 3 to 5 minutes until light and fluffy.

Guemes Guruchew

Here is an extraordinary healthful treat, offered by our friend and resident island artist, Zobra Anasazi. These are an ideal snack for your next biking or kayaking trip through the islands.

1 pound toasted whole almonds
1 pound raw sunflower seeds
1 pound sesame seeds
1½ cups honey

1. Remove almond skins: Place almonds in boiling water for about 1 minute or until skins slip off easily. Drain and pat dry; place in large bowl.

2. Preheat oven to 300°. Stir remaining ingredients into the bowl; mix well. Pour onto a greased 11 x 16-inch rimmed baking sheet.

3. Bake for 15 minutes and stir. Continue cooking for about 1 hour more, stirring every 15 minutes or until mixture is golden brown and thickened.

4. Remove from oven and turn out onto large sheet of buttered heavy foil. Spread mixture into a thin but compact layer. Set aside to cool.

5. When cool, break into pieces. Store in a covered container.   6 cups

Banana Nut Cake

This old-fashioned favorite is so easy to make. It is a deliciously moist cake, perfect for backyard picnics.

½ cup margarine or butter
1 cup sugar
2 eggs
1 teaspoon vanilla extract
2 very ripe bananas, sliced
2¼ cups unbleached white flour
1¼ teaspoons baking soda
1 teaspoon salt
½ cup buttermilk
¾ cup coarsely chopped walnuts
CREAM CHEESE FROSTING (recipe follows)
¼ cup finely chopped walnuts, toasted

1. Preheat oven to 350°. In a large mixing bowl, cream together margarine and sugar. Beat in eggs and vanilla, mixing well. Add bananas and beat again.

2. On low speed, beat in flour, soda and salt to egg mixture. Add buttermilk and mix; stir in nuts.

3. Pour into a greased and floured 9 X 13-inch baking pan. Bake for 30 to 35 minutes or until toothpick inserted in center of cake comes out clean. Remove from oven and place on a wire rack to cool.

4. Prepare Cream Cheese Frosting. When cool, frost cake and sprinkle with toasted walnuts.   1 9x13-inch cake

CREAM CHEESE FROSTING
1 (3-ounce) package cream cheese
2 tablespoons margarine or butter
1 teaspoon vanilla
1 ½ cups powdered sugar
1 tablespoon milk, as needed

In a medium bowl, mix together cream cheese, margarine and vanilla. Gradually beat in sugar until mixture is smooth and easily spread. Add milk to thin, if necessary.

Chocolate Walnut Supremes

Holly B's Bakery on Lopez Island is where islanders and visitors alike congregate to enjoy fresh baked bread, pastries and desserts along with a cup of coffee and a warm, friendly atmosphere. These rich bar cookies are typical of her delicious fare.

Filling
>   9 ounces sweetened condensed milk
>   1⅛ cups semi-sweet chocolate chips
>   1¼ tablespoons butter
>   ⅛ teaspoon salt
>   ½ teaspoon vanilla extract

Dough
>   5 ounces butter
>   1¼ cups packed brown sugar
>   ¾ teaspoon instant coffee granules
>   ¾ teaspoon vanilla extract
>   2 medium eggs
>   1⅞ cups rolled oats
>   1¼ cups coarsely chopped walnuts
>   1⅝ cups all-purpose flour
>   ¾ teaspoon baking soda
>   ¼ teaspoon salt

1. Prepare filling: In a microwave-safe bowl, combine filling ingredients. Cook 30 seconds and stir to blend; continue cooking until chocolate has melted. Set aside to cool slightly.

2. Preheat oven to 400°. Prepare dough: In a large mixing bowl, cream butter and sugar until fluffy. Mix in remaining dough ingredients. Set aside 1 cup of dough. Press remaining dough into a buttered jelly-roll pan.

3. Spread filling over top of dough. Crumble reserved dough over filling as evenly as possible.

4. Place pan in center of the oven and bake about 15 minutes or until top is slightly browned. Remove from oven and cool on wire racks. Cut into bars.   16 bar cookies

Fidalgo Island Chocolate Mousse

Derek Beck's mousse is a fabulous experience for anyone who enjoys the smooth, sweet, rich flavor of chocolate. It is only one of the outstanding desserts waiting for you at La Petite Restaurant on Fidalgo Island.

½ cup sugar
¼ cup water
8 ounces bittersweet chocolate, broken into small pieces
3 tablespoons Grand Marnier liqueur
2½ cups whipping cream

1. In a pan, over medium heat, dissolve sugar in water to make a simple syrup. Remove from heat and set aside.

2. In a heavy-bottomed saucepan, over low heat, melt chocolate. Add Grand Marnier to chocolate. Carefully ignite liqueur; it will flame briefly, burning off excess alcohol.

3. Slowly add simple syrup to chocolate mixture, stirring continuously until smooth. Remove from heat, and allow to cool for 20 minutes.

4. In a large mixing bowl, whip cream until it just begins to hold shape. Stir 1/2 cup whipped cream into cooled chocolate mixture; fold mixture back into remaining whipped cream. Fold gently, until just blended.

5. Spoon into individual parfait glasses. Cover and refrigerate until set, about 2 hours.

4 servings

Chocolate Macaroons

These chewy cookies will melt in your mouth.

3 ounces unsweetened chocolate
4 egg whites, room temperature
½ teaspoon salt
1½ cups sugar
2 tablespoons unbleached white flour
1 teaspoon vanilla extract
3 cups shredded coconut

1. Preheat oven to 325°. In a small bowl, melt chocolate in microwave; set aside.

2. In a large mixing bowl, beat egg whites until foamy. In a small bowl combine salt, sugar and flour. Gradually add sugar mixture to egg whites, beating continuously until mixture holds stiff peaks. Stir in vanilla and melted chocolate. Gently fold in coconut.

3. Line a large baking sheet with parchment paper. Using a teaspoon, drop batter onto paper. Bake for 20 minutes. Remove from oven and allow to cool for 5 minutes. Using a spatula, transfer cookies to a wire rack. Store in covered container when cooled.   2 dozen cookies

Ginger Spice Cookies

With a view of Turtleback Mountain on Orcas Island, Turtleback Farm Inn provides a sanctuary of quiet respite. It offers an atmosphere of tranquil hospitality as well as heart-warming food. We think you will enjoy the Inn's rich, snappy butter cookies.

1½ cups butter
2 cups brown sugar
½ cup molasses
2 eggs
4 cups all-purpose flour
4 teaspoons baking soda
2 teaspoons ground ginger
2 teaspoons ground cloves
2 teaspoons cinnamon
½ teaspoon salt
1 cup rolled oats
½ cup currants or raisins
¾ cup chopped nuts

1. Preheat oven to 375°. In mixing bowl, blend butter, sugar and molasses. Mix in eggs, one at a time, until creamy.

2. Add flour, baking soda, spices and salt to egg mixture; beat until flour has been absorbed. Using a large spoon, blend in oats, currants and nuts.

3. With a teaspoon, drop batter onto greased cookie sheet. Bake for 12 to 15 minutes or until lightly browned. Remove from oven and transfer cookies onto metal racks to cool.   5 dozen cookies

Juliet's Kisses

This recipe comes to us from Chef Michael Magerkurth, of Geppetto's in Anacortes, on Fidalgo Island. He sampled these cookie kisses, named after Juliet Montague of *Romeo and Juliet* fame, while in Verona, Italy.

1 scant cup finely chopped almonds or hazelnuts, divided
½ pound unsalted butter, softened
½ cup powdered sugar
¼ teaspoon salt
1 teaspoon vanilla extract
1⅔ cups all-purpose flour
⅓ cup Dutch cocoa powder, sifted
Filling
    2 ounces semi-sweet chocolate
    2 teaspoons unsalted butter

1. Preheat oven to 350°. Place nuts in a shallow baking dish and bake for 5 minutes or until lightly toasted. Remove from oven and set aside to cool.

2. In a large bowl, cream butter and sugar until fluffy. Mix in salt, vanilla, flour, cocoa and 1/2 cup nuts. Shape dough into 3/4-inch balls.

3. Place balls on ungreased cookie sheet about 1 inch apart. Bake about 10 to 12 minutes, or until golden. Remove from oven and cool on wire racks.

4. Prepare filling: In a double boiler, melt chocolate and butter. With a whisk blend in remaining nuts. Remove from heat.

5. To make sandwich kisses: Place one teaspoon of filling on bottom of cookie and place a second cookie bottom over filling. Repeat procedure with remaining cookies and filling.   2 dozen

Holiday Mincefruit Squares

These fruit-filled cookies have become one of our favorite holiday treats. Prepare the mincefruit filling ahead of time and refrigerate or freeze until needed.

> MINCEFRUIT FILLING (recipe follows)
> 2½ cups flour
> 1 tablespoon sugar
> 1 teaspoon salt
> 1 cup butter or margarine
> 1 egg, separated
> Milk
> 3 tablespoons powdered sugar
> 1 tablespoon lemon juice

1. Prepare Mincefruit Filling.

2. Preheat oven to 400°. In a large bowl, sift together flour, sugar and salt. With a pastry blender or fork, cut in butter or margarine until mixture resembles coarse meal.

3. Beat egg yolk in measuring cup and add enough milk to measure 1/2 cup. Add to flour mixture and toss until mixture is evenly moistened. Form into a ball and divide dough in half.

4. On a lightly floured board, roll one half of the dough out to measure 11 x 15 inches. Carefully transfer to a large ungreased baking sheet. Spread 3 cups of mincefruit filling to within 3/4-inch of edge.

5. Roll out second half of dough and place on top, crimp edges to seal. In a small bowl, beat egg white stiff; brush over dough.

6. Bake for 25 minutes or until golden. Remove baking sheet from oven and place on a rack to cool.

7. In a small bowl, combine powdered sugar and lemon juice. While still hot, drizzle icing over pastry. Cut into 2-inch squares; serve while warm or store in a covered container.

30 squares

MINCEFRUIT FILLING
This recipe will make two batches of Mincefruit Squares.

  2 pounds pears, peeled
  1½ pounds apples, peeled
  2 medium oranges, unpeeled
  2 cups seedless raisins
  2½ cups sugar
  2 teaspoons cinnamon
  1½ teaspoons cloves
  1½ teaspoons salt

1. Cut fruit into quarters, remove cores and seeds. Using a knife or food processor, cut fruit into 1/2-inch squares.

2. In a large pot, place chopped fruit and remaining ingredients; stir to combine. Over medium-high heat, bring fruit mixture to a boil.

3. Reduce heat and simmer until thick, about 2 hours, stirring often. Remove from heat, cover and refrigerate or freeze.   6 cups

Tiramisu

Italian for "pick me up," Tiramisu is a sinfully rich dessert of brandy-and-coffee soaked ladyfingers stacked between layers of mascarpone (an Italian sweetened cream cheese) and whipped cream filling.

    2 teaspoons instant coffee granules
    ¾ cup boiling water
    4 to 6 tablespoons brandy or cognac
    1 (6-ounce) package crisp Italian lady finger cookies*
    4 large egg yolks
    1 cup sugar
    10 ounces mascarpone* (1¼ cups)
    1 ¾ cups whipping cream
    3 ounces dark chocolate shavings, garnish

1. In a small bowl, stir together coffee and boiling water; allow to cool. Stir in brandy.

2. In a 9 x 13-inch baking dish, arrange half the lady fingers and drizzle with half of the coffee mixture.

3. In a mixing bowl, beat egg yolks and sugar until thick and lemon-colored. Pour mixture into the top of a double boiler over simmering water. Stirring constantly, cook 8 to 10 minutes. Remove from heat and whisk in mascarpone; beat until smooth.

4. In a large mixing bowl, beat whipping cream until it holds soft peaks; fold into the cheese mixture.

5. Spoon half of the cream filling over the first layer of lady fingers. Layer the remaining lady fingers on top and drizzle with remaining coffee mixture. Top with remaining cream filling. Sprinkle with chocolate shavings.

6. Cover and chill at least 8 hours.   12 servings

*Available in Italian specialty markets.

Calico Bread Pudding

The three Calico Cupboard Cafes located in Skagit Valley are owned by Linda Freed and have become something of a local legend. Known for quality cuisine and baked goods, they feature an eclectic blend of comfort foods and Northwest fare. Everything is made the old-fashioned way, from scratch.

    4 slices white or French bread
    4 slices whole wheat bread
    ¼ cup soft butter
    ⅔ cup brown sugar
    1 tablespoon cinnamon
    ¾ cup raisins
    ¾ cup finely chopped apple
    2½ cups milk
    2½ cups light cream
    6 eggs
    1 tablespoon vanilla extract
    ⅔ cup sugar
    Whipped cream, garnish

1. Preheat oven to 350°. Remove crusts from bread and discard or reserve for another use. Toast bread and spread with butter. Top with brown sugar and cinnamon. Cut bread into bite-size pieces.

2. In a buttered 2-quart glass baking dish, layer bread cubes, raisins and chopped apple, alternating layers. Set aside.

3. In a medium saucepan, over medium-high heat, scald milk and cream. Set aside.

4. In a bowl, beat eggs; add vanilla and sugar. Stir scalded milk and cream into egg mixture and pour over bread and fruit in baking dish. Place baking dish in a pan with hot water, 1-inch deep.

5. Bake pudding for about 1 hour or until knife inserted in the middle comes out clean. Serve pudding warm, garnished with whipped cream.

6-8 servings

Double Chocolate Walnut Biscotti

Rosario Resort, on Orcas Island, is listed on the National Register of Historic Places. It is one of our region's premier resorts. Savor these decadent biscotti with red wine or coffee in the mansion's elegant dining room, enjoying the view over the terraced pool and across to Lopez Island.

1 cup coarsely chopped walnuts
6 eggs
1½ teaspoons vanilla extract
2⅔ cups all-purpose flour
2 cups sugar
1 tablespoon baking soda
¼ teaspoon salt
1 tablespoon instant Espresso powder
4 ounces bittersweet chocolate chips
1 cup Dutch process cocoa powder

1. Preheat oven to 325°. Place walnuts in a shallow baking dish and bake for 8 minutes or until nuts are lightly browned. Remove from oven and set aside to cool. With a large knife, coarsely chop walnuts and set aside.

2. In a medium bowl, whisk eggs and vanilla together until incorporated; set aside. In a large mixing bowl, combine remaining ingredients; stir in walnuts. Slowly add eggs and vanilla; mix until blended.

3. Line two large baking sheets with parchment. Divide dough into fourths and place on a floured board. Roll each portion into an oval log about 2 inches wide and 12 inches long.

4. Place logs on parchment and bake for 20 minutes. Remove from oven and let cool about 10 minutes.

5. Reduce oven heat to 300°. Place logs on a cutting board. Using a serrated knife, cut the logs diagonally into 1/2-inch slices. Lay biscotti on baking sheet and bake for 8 minutes; turn biscotti and continue baking 8 minutes more.

6. Remove baking sheet from oven and transfer the biscotti to a rack to cool. Biscotti can be stored in an airtight container for up to 1 month.

3 dozen

Almond Biscotti

The Italian word, biscotti, means twice-cooked. June Bisordi serves these fragrant, crunchy cookies in the evening with wine or coffee. When these cookies are baking, the licorice aroma of the anise permeates the house welcoming family or friends.

    1 cup whole almonds
    ½ cup butter
    1 cup granulated sugar
    3 eggs
    ½ teaspoon vanilla extract
    2¾ cups all-purpose flour
    1½ teaspoons baking powder
    ¼ teaspoon salt
    1½ teaspoons ground anise seed

1. Preheat oven to 350°. Place almonds in a shallow baking dish and bake for 8 minutes or until lightly browned. Remove from oven and set aside to cool. With a large knife, coarsely chop almonds and set aside.

2. In a mixing bowl, cream butter and sugar together until fluffy. Add eggs, beating them in one at a time. Mix in vanilla and set aside.

3. Sift together flour, baking powder, salt and anise. Add sifted dry ingredients and chopped almonds to butter mixture and mix until blended. Be careful not to overmix. Cover dough with plastic wrap and refrigerate for 2 to 3 hours.

4. Preheat oven to 350°. Remove dough from refrigerator, divide in half and place on a floured board. Roll each half into an oval log about 2 inches wide and 12 inches long. Place logs on a greased baking sheet. Place baking sheet in center of oven and bake for 25 minutes, until dough has risen slightly and is lightly browned. Remove from oven and let cool about 10 minutes.

5. Place logs on a cutting board. Using a serrated knife, cut the logs diagonally into 1/2-inch slices. Lay the biscotti on baking sheet and bake again until golden brown, about 10 minutes. Remove from oven and transfer the biscotti to a rack to cool. Biscotti can be stored in an airtight container for up to 1 month.   3 dozen biscotti

Hazelnut Orange Biscotti

For an added treat, dip one end of each biscotti into melted chocolate.

¾ cup whole hazelnuts
⅓ cup butter
¾ cup sugar
2 eggs
1 teaspoon vanilla extract
½ teaspoon orange extract
2 teaspoons grated orange zest
2¼ cups all-purpose flour
1½ teaspoons baking powder
⅛ teaspoon nutmeg
¼ teaspoon salt

1. Preheat oven to 350°. Place hazelnuts in a shallow baking dish and bake for 8 minutes. Remove from oven and set aside to cool. With a large knife, coarsely chop hazelnuts and set aside.

2. In a mixing bowl, cream butter and sugar together until fluffy. Add eggs, beating them in one at a time. Mix in vanilla, orange extract and zest; set aside.

3. In a bowl, combine, flour, baking powder, nutmeg and salt. Add dry ingredients to butter mixture and mix until blended. Stir nuts into batter.

4. Preheat oven to 325°. Divide dough in half and place on floured board. Roll each half into an oval log about 1/2 inch high, 2 inches wide and 12 inches long. Place logs on a greased baking sheet about 2 inches apart.

5. Place baking sheet in center of oven and bake for 25 minutes, until dough has risen slightly and is lightly browned. Remove from oven and allow to cool about 5 minutes.

6. Place logs on a cutting board. Using a serrated knife, cut the logs diagonally, at a 45° angle, into 1/2-inch slices. Lay the biscotti on baking sheet and bake for 5 minutes, turn biscotti and continue baking 5 minutes more, or until golden brown.

7. Remove from oven and transfer the biscotti to a rack to cool. Biscotti can be stored in an airtight container for up to 1 month.   3 1/2 dozen biscotti

Index

Ginger Spice Cookies, 276
Northwest Eggs, 223
Pacific Rim Mussels, 141
Tuscan Chicken with Garbanzo Beans, 81

V

Vegetables/Side Dishes
Bistro Potatoes, 185
Classic Risotto, 191
Chantrelle Risotto Cakes, 192-193
Creamed Onions, 184
Fiery Broccoli, 179
Five-Spice Basmati Rice, 194
Garlic Mashed Potatoes, 187
Gingered Vegetables in Black Bean Sauce, 201
Harvest Corn, 181
Herb Roasted Vegetables, 182-183
Mike's Noodle Stir-Fry, 195
Oven-Roasted Asparagus, 180
Polenta, 197
Porcini Mushroom Sauce, 198
Potato Latkes, 190
Roasted Eggplant, 200
Roasted Potatoes with Rosemary, 186
Sesame and Ginger Noodles, 196
Stir-Fried Asparagus with Sesame Seeds, 180
Sweet and Sour Baked Beans, 199
Sweet Potato Gnocchi, 188
Yams with Orange Butter, 189

W

Walser Farms
Blueberry Peach Pie, 264
Sweet Cheese Blintzes, 230
Watermelon Strawberry Sorbet, 234
Westcott Bay Sea Farms
Pete's Barbecued Oysters, 27
White Chocolate Ice Cream With Blackberry
Sauce in, 254
Wild Blackberry Cobbler, 265
Wild Rice Hazelnut Salad, 74
Windsong Bed and Breakfast
Apple Oat Cereal, 234
Watermelon Strawberry Sorbet, 234

Y

Yams with Orange Butter, 189

Z

Zesty Chicken, 82